joy!

joy!

by Barbara Evans
Correspondence
with
PAT BOONE

Creation House, Carol Stream, Illinois

ACKNOWLEDGMENT

Bible quotations are taken from *New American Standard Bible* by permission of Lockman Foundation, La Habra, California.

First Edition

JOY Copyright © 1973 by Creation House, Inc. All rights reserved. Printed in the United States of America. No part of this book may be used or reproduced in any manner whatsoever without written permission of the publisher except in the case of brief quotations in articles and reviews. For information address Creation House, Incorporated, 499 Gunderson Drive, Carol Stream, Illinois 60187.

Library of Congress Catalog Card Number: 72-94923
ISBN 0-88419-060-9

contents

INTRODUCTION

For ten years of my life I was a lesbian.

The summer after my graduation from high school I was introduced to the gay life in my home town of Hartford, Connecticut. During Christmas vacation in my freshman year in college, I attended a gay party and was "married" to my lover.

We were not the bar-hopping, carousing type, but a quiet law-abiding couple. Many of our gay group attended church and church functions regularly.

The social events we attended were held in the homes of other lesbians or homosexuals. For the most part the group would be made up of "married" couples, although several singles might also be present. Most of us were professional people: teachers, nurses, lawyers, businessmen and women.

While there was unfaithfulness to our mates from time to time, I do not believe it was any more so than among heterosexual couples. But our "married" relationships did suffer with time. Most so-called marriages lasted only three to four years. This meant that there was a good bit of exchanging going on among many of our gay acquaintances. While we laughed and joked about it when we got together, it often led to deep emotional crises and to several suicides.

Did I really enjoy this life? I thought so, for not since my junior year in high school had I been interested in men.

From the time I entered adolescence my father had warned me to beware of the male animal. He criticized the boys in whom I showed an interest as a young teenager. He even criticized physicians. "They've gotten into the profession so they can have fun examining nude women."

My mother was kind and loving. But because my younger brother had a continuing illness, she was forced to devote much of her time to him. As a result, I really had no one to whom I could turn in my adolescent years —except my music teacher.

And she was the one who became my lover.

Then one day I picked up a movie magazine which published an excerpt from Pat Boone's book, *A New Song*. Pat Boone had been a favorite of mine during my high school days, but I had lost track of him since then. Now the article showed pictures of his wife and four daughters. I was intrigued and bought the book at a bookstore near the campus.

With nothing to do on July 4th I sat down to read it. Never before do I remember reading an entire book at one sitting. This one I did. Something in what Pat said spoke to me. I began to have all kinds of doubts about the life I was leading.

One thought persisted. *Get in touch with Pat Boone. He can help you.*

So I called long distance, and his secretary said he would answer my letter if I wrote. I didn't believe he would, but he did though I signed a fictitious name. And how I thank God for the new life which He has given to me as a result. For the first time in my life I know what it is to be happy—really happy.

Barbara Evans

Hartford, Conn.

P.S. I have two prayers concerning this account of God's dealing with me. First, that those involved in my past will in no way be hurt.

Second, and most important, I pray that in some way this story will encourage others who may be involved in the gay life to seek the love of Jesus, and in this search find God's power to change their lives.

Editor's Note: To protect the reputation of Barbara Evans and her friends, both the names and locations are fictitious.

PREFACE

"These things have I spoken unto you, that My joy may be in you, and *that your joy may be made full.*" (John 15:11)

"Until now you have asked for nothing in My name; ask, and you will receive, that your joy may be made full." (John 16:24)

1

gay and happy aren't the same

Dear Pat Boone:

I have read your book and nothing has ever hit me quite so hard. You see, my problem is unusual, although being in the entertainment world, you've probably run across it.

I belong to the gay world, and what I do at this point very definitely affects another person.

Although I had a very devout and religious attitude when I was younger (against my parents' wishes), I became very fond of a high school teacher. Then in my junior year an older man whom I had been dating regularly suddenly showed up in church with his wife. I was completely broken and fell back upon my teacher friend.

The summer before I entered college this friendship developed into a homosexual relationship. I went through six or seven periods of moving in and out because my friend was concerned over our age differences (twenty-one years). This did not deter me. Earlier when I had been in close connection with the church, I prayed that God would let love come to us. At that time, I could see no wrong—now I honestly don't know.

I have not attended church anywhere regularly. I am a music teacher and love my work. By the way, I'm also a singer of sorts, and that's one of the ways in which I have been involved in the church. I have a few students who take private lessons with me, and I have encouraged them to participate in church activities.

Well, I'm not giving you my good side against my bad side. I just can't seem to sort things out properly. I am a 27-year-old graduate student, but I can't answer these questions. What hope is there for me? Can I continue to love another woman whom I practically compelled to love me? Does God say there is one and only one way to live?

I felt if anyone would know where to seek help, you would. I know I should go to God, but I'm so afraid. It could mean a change in my way of living, and that could destroy someone else's life. You see, one of our gay group had some kind of religious experience and now she lives alone.

My friend has read your book and knows I'm upset. But, we've both read similar accounts. *This just got to me.* I've tried to convince my friend that my love is still the same, but I haven't even convinced myself.

By the way, we are not the carousing, bar-hopping type. We lead a very quiet life and have a few other gay friends, but still I don't know what could happen. I guess somehow I hope that God can accept me and let me remain with my roommate.

I don't know what else to tell you. You may consider this letter a waste of your valuable time. I hope not.

Of course due to the situation at home and my very private life against my very public life, please send anything in care of General Delivery. You may not even wish to answer, but after reading your book, I had to write. I'm so confused even rereading my letter.

Hopefully,

Joy Carol

July 16

Dear Joy:

Joy, your letter has really had an impact upon me. I've had other letters from people with similar problems, but I really detect in you an earnestness and an honesty and a genuine desire to be in the center of God's will. I *know* that He has heard your request and knows your heart and will draw you perfectly to Him. I think the fact that your letter got to me is just one indication of the way He's working in your life.

As I was reading your letter a Scripture verse came to my mind. I looked it up and found it in Deuteronomy, chapter 30, beginning with verse 11. I think it would be good to read from there on to the end of the chapter, but the special passage that came into my mind was in verse 14, "But the word is very near you, *in your mouth and in your heart*, that you may do it."

Throughout your letter there is the indication in your own words that you realize something is wrong, out of kilter, not in balance in your life, and you're wanting very much for your life to be close to God and ordered as He would have it.

Now jump into chapter 10 of Romans beginning with verse 8 and read through verse 11 or even into verse 13.

Notice that Paul was familiar with this spiritual prin-

13

ciple that Moses had written in Deuteronomy, and he brought it right up to date and into the Christian time there in chapter 10 of Romans.

Verse 10 is especially important to you: "For with the heart man believes, resulting in righteousness, *and with the mouth he confesses, resulting in salvation.*" That spiritual principle is just as alive today as when Paul first uttered it, and it's already operating in your life! It has caused you to write the letter; it has caused the letter to get to me; and now my answer comes back to you. But the best part is that *God has known the desire of your heart* and is honoring the confession of your mouth.

Isn't that exciting?

Joy, I'm not a preacher, and I'm no great Christian. I'm just a human being who has come to understand a little bit of God's love and power for us today.

I want you to know that I do not judge or condemn you in any way. As you already read in my book, I slipped into all kinds of sin and it nearly wrecked my life. I thought I had good reasons for it, and a lot of it seemed harmless and even very good for me and the other people involved. But gradually, like a cancer, it was destroying everything that was really precious to me and making it impossible for me to function as I was meant by God to function—and therefore robbing me of the only real happiness that there is in this life.

As you already read, I found that all the answers to every one of my problems was supplied by Jesus as I totally surrendered my life and my will to Him.

I have to repeat this process every day and remind myself and my very real enemy, Satan, that I want Jesus to control my life and to work in me "both to will and to work for His good pleasure" (according to Philippians 2:12-13). That last verse has become very exciting to me now because it allows me to put the burden on God to cause me to want to do His will—and then to do it. He says He will, and He will!

May I suggest a couple of things? I wish I knew someone to recommend to you, but at the moment I can't think of anybody. However, I'm taking a personal interest in you from this moment on because I earnestly believe that God is going to do some miraculous things in your life. I want you to write me as things begin to develop.

First, if you don't have one already, please get a current version of the New Testament. I suggest *Living New Testament, Good News for Modern Man,* or *The New Testament in Modern English* translated by J. B. Phillips. All of them bring the Scriptures to life in today's language. It really was a great breakthrough to hear Jesus speaking to me in words that I use myself all the time. The truths are the same; they never change.

The second is a rugged one. I believe our malicious enemy, Satan, has gotten quite a grip on your emotions, your senses, and even your thinking process. You have felt this and cried out for help. He doesn't want you to have it and *will block it any way he can.*

So I suggest you do what Paul did in Acts 9, verse 9: *fast for three days, praying just as often as you can during that time.* If you have to work, that's all right, but try not to have any company at all with the people who would keep you drawn into this gay world. It won't be easy. If I know the devil, he will tempt you in every way he can during that three-day period, causing some of your friends to find you wherever you are, and to tempt you with perhaps the strongest temptations you've ever faced.

But if you're fasting and praying and reading the words of Jesus you'll be strong, and His Spirit will sustain you. At the end of that three days I believe that you will have come to recognize your enemy and also to have a very keen sense of the presence of the Lord with you.

Do you have the courage to enter into such an elemental struggle as this? If you do, Jesus will be with you.

Joy, sweet sister, our enemy is real! It is not your love for your friends—male and female—that is wrong and destructive; it's the sensual element that Satan has woven into it, taking advantage of mutual weaknesses and mutual emotional scars and twisting them into something destructive to you and to your friends.

Jesus won't ask you to give up your love for them; but He will purify it and make it constructive and helpful for their sakes, for yours and for His own sake.

You see, He died for your friend just as He died for you and me, and He loves them and perhaps will help them eternally through you. You can't help them, no matter how much you may want to, but He can, and will. Read Ephesians 6, beginning with verse 10 and through verse 17. You're in for a battle, so you might as well know the nature of it and the weapons at your command. Also read James 4, beginning with verse 7 through verse 10. This is a blueprint for action and a battle plan for victory.

I also believe that before that three-day period of fasting and prayer is over the Lord will have brought someone to you who can be a continuing source of spiritual strength. I have no idea who it will be, but He does. Test Him; try Him; let Him prove to you personally and intimately how wrapped up He is in your life and how well He knows your needs. This will be the most exciting adventure of your life, Joy.

Meanwhile, I'll be praying for you and claiming the victory that I know God will bring into your life if you'll just turn it over to Him. Thanks for writing me and for giving me the opportunity to share in this adventure that you have already begun.

Your brother in Jesus,

Pat Boone

PB:jef

16

P.S. Not long ago I baptized a young Jewish woman, mother of four, wife of a successful Baltimore lawyer. After reading A NEW SONG (and several other books) she said, "I have just fallen in love with Jesus! I know that he is the Messiah!" On the way to her baptism, she said very earnestly, "I'm so excited—I feel like I'm about to be married!" And, of course, I assured her that she was. This feeling is valid and I'm certain very precious to God. In the Bible, we as a church and as individuals are pictured being married to Jesus. Once this union has really become a reality in your life old things will have passed away, and all things will become new! (2 Corinthians 5:17)

Pat

2

something is happening!

Dear Pat:

I hope you don't mind my calling you Pat—I feel as though you are a very dear friend. I don't know where to begin to tell you some of the things that have happened to me.

First, after I read your book, I waited awhile to write to you and I almost didn't. But somehow I knew I just had to.

Every other day I stopped to see if there was a letter. I had almost given up.

Now I have read and reread every word.

The Scripture was no problem and I already have a modern English translation. But staying away from my gay friends—especially the one I live with—is difficult.

I'm doing graduate work this summer. Since school started I've been looking for a girl by the name of Joan that I met several years ago who I was sure was a Christian. I hadn't thought much about her, but Monday, after reading your letter—*there was Joan in my workshop.* I've talked with her very little, because I still don't know what I'm doing. *I only know that something is happening to me.* So I asked if I could spend the weekend at her country home—so I am going to get away.

My response to my friend to whom I am "married" has not been the same the last two days, and I'm sure she senses a wall between us. I just can't help it. But this morning I almost said I couldn't go this weekend. But then I remembered your letter; I know I must.

Another thing, I had continued my reading until last night. Monday I read and finished Acts, practically devouring everything I could. I started Romans, and when I read the part starting from Romans 1:18—on to the end of the chapter—I was literally shocked into a realization. How could I have missed this when I was searching so many years ago?

Oh, I want God's help so much. It's so hard for me to believe that God is working to help me, but *something is happening.*

I'm so afraid I'll turn back, and yet I know I can't.

Please continue to pray for me. I've got to make it! I've just got to.

If you write again, for now you should continue to send it to General Delivery, but I would like you to know that my real name is Barbara Evans.

And, Pat, I just may owe God my life because of you!

Prayerfully,

Barbara

P.S. It's the next day. School's over, and I'm on my

way home. I'm so tired; I feel weak. I know I haven't eaten much all week. You are right; our enemy is at work—I just want to return home to the comfort of my friend. But I'm trying to have courage—I've got to make it!

August 4

Dear Barbara:

You can imagine that I was thrilled to receive your last letter letting me know that you had already done the things that I recommended in my letter of a couple days before. God truly has our thoughts and spirits moving in the same direction. Praise His name!

I really get goose bumps reading your letter and realizing that God has truly taken a hand in your life and will perform the miracles that you want Him to. How thankful I am that "He touched me."

I prayed for your friend, as well, and thank God for her sensitivity to the Lord's leading. I'm sure that before too long the Boone family will be doing a concert in or around Hartford and we'll see you in person.

We do continue to pray for you and I recommend that you read in your Bible *the short book of Jude.*

Your brother in Jesus,

Pat Boone

PB:jef

3

God, help me!

Dear Pat:

I made it! There was only one thing I could do after the first seed was planted. I had to get away and I did. So much has happened and is continuing to happen.

I can't begin to describe the feeling I have. Some things are tremendously painful, but I have a complete trust in God and have (as you were sure would happen) a feeling of His presence in my life.

I'd like to tell you what happened.

On Thursday evening when I got home from school, my roommate seemed to know that something was not right between us. After a short conversation, I had confirmed her fears. Of course, she was very shaken. But she did not try to stop me from going.

I got everything ready, and leaving Friday morning was a very difficult thing. She said she knew that once I started this, I would go all the way.

I left, and at school the day went rather quickly. Joan and I set out for her home in the evening. I had—and still have—such a feeling of expectancy. It was raining very hard on the way and I drove. When I finally got to bed I didn't sleep much. I had been "hit in the face" so hard by the passage of scripture in Romans.

Saturday, I got away by myself. I took my Bible and your book and letter. I needed all the courage and encouragement I could manage.

I walked down by the stream where I found a big rock—big enough to climb up and lie down. There I read and prayed and meditated. I thought of so many things. After spending most of the day on that rock, I began to walk back to the house. As I was walking through the field, my heart became so heavy, I kneeled and cried and prayed. I had come to the realization that I wanted God to take over my life—*no matter what!*

That night in bed I read and prayed again. I had an even greater sense of God's presence. I asked for healing and guidance, yielding my life completely to God's service.

Sunday I went to church with an unusual invisible presence around me.

Well, Pat, I want you to know that when the service began, I knew there was *no way I could turn away.* How could I partake of communion with God and return to something I had been totally convinced in my own heart was wrong? It was not possible. Oh, thank God for Christian people like my school chum. Although she could in no way take away the pain of realizing my sinfulness, she put her arm around me as I openly cried during the prayer and communion hymn. There was no other way. Thank God that He has been so patient with me.

In the afternoon I went back to the church to talk to the minister.

When I first wrote to you it was very hard to express my problem. But with the sense of the presence of God, it seemed much easier to talk to this minister. I told him what had happened and the problem in my life. He, like you, did not try to condemn me. But being able to translate both Greek and Hebrew he indicated to me that what I already thought or knew was true.

He gave me encouragement and said that now a most difficult decision was ahead—that only I could choose. I had to decide about what to do with my situation. I told him that I wanted God to have His way in my life. He said it was going to be painful, and it is!

Sunday evening I went with Joan and her husband to a black church service. Their church, a small-town congregation, is sponsoring a white ministerial student to help the congregation in its evangelism. Everything in the service seemed to touch me. "Do not be ashamed of the Gospel" was the text, and I sat there intently listening to the Jamaican minister preach from Romans 1:16. Even the solos were an inspiration and fire to my heart. Sunday night seemed to pass quickly and I was secure in the feeling I had had before: that *God will take care of everything*.

Monday, I was anxious to be on my way, because I knew that ahead of me lay the most difficult and painful confrontation with my "friend."

Although the minister had said not to tell Joan about myself, she had confided something very close and personal about herself to me. And as the weekend had progressed I became more and more confident of her true Christian friendship. She and her family were just wonderful to me. So, on the way back to school I told her. It shocked her only briefly. She accepted it, and I'm sure genuinely understood in light of other things that she knew about my home life. She did not really know that it was dealt with plainly in the Bible. I told her where to read and she did as we were driving. She offered me her home as a refuge anytime and to share her trailer while at school if I needed to get away immediately. She prayed with me, and her friendship has to be one of God's richest blessings!

I went to classes yesterday and then immediately home. I could have waited, but a certain magnetism seemed to draw me toward the confrontation as soon as was possible.

Yesterday and last night were almost a nightmare, but I can rejoice in God's love. Only He could have helped me. My "friend" gave me many arguments because she really doesn't understand. She says she feels God's will in her life, too, and she doesn't believe that you have to give up a love for someone else. So, I told her, it's there in black and white. For me I have no other choice. She said she really had expected this, but what threw her was my wanting to move right away.

I finally told her that I could *not* stay.

She made no attempt to persuade me to change my decision to live for God, but I don't see how that would be totally possible if I were to stay. Of course, she is right about the practical side of my telling other people about the situation, but I believe in God's power, and He can still protect her even though He demands my life on His terms. She is so afraid of losing her job.

I also went to our neighbors (a gay couple) and told them of my decision. I expected ridicule but they were understanding. They offered their help and told me to keep in touch.

The blow really came with this very dear friend of mine who is one of the "gay" gang—not tied to anyone—but searching. I was in hopes that he would be especially receptive and it might be helpful to him. I have loved him as a friend for many years. We have gone through much suffering together. He was the most skeptical. He feels as if this has happened too suddenly and that I've "gone off the deep end." He didn't talk to me maliciously but he certainly couldn't understand my decision.

Now, my friend (or I should say former friend) and all my close gay associates know. My biggest problem is about the moving. And I want to get involved in God's work.

Pat, I don't know where I go from here. But I am totally confident that wherever it is, God is going to lead. Although I feel the presence of God around me, I still feel that my joy cannot be complete until I am completely free from my old life. And I don't see how I can feel completely free until I move. But I'm just taking one day, one hour at a time.

Please continue to pray for me. I'm not standing firm yet—but I will be! Someday I'd like to come out and meet you and your family and rejoice with you for this great revelation of God's love and will in my life.

I know that you have a very busy life, but I'll appreciate it if you write. I thank God that you somehow were allowed to communicate with me the first time. I believe in miracles, too. For, if God can take someone like me, whom psychologists say it is next to impossible to change, and change my life—then I know God can do anything!

I pray God's blessing upon you and your family as you continue your work in His will.

With love, a true sister in Christ,

Barbara Evans

August 15

Dear Barbara:

I hope to make this a quick and brief letter, because I feel it's urgent. I praise God for the way He has moved

27

into your life and is literally taking you by the hand! *Don't let go!!*

Normally, I'm not an emotional person, but I'll admit tears came to my eyes as I read the way God brought just the right people across your path and the influence to bear upon you. In Proverbs 21, the first couple of verses, we learn that "the King's heart is in the hand of the Lord, as the rivers of water; he turns it wherever he wishes." I don't have it in front of me, but the indication is that God digs irrigation channels, and although the water is free and active, it moves in the channels He has prepared for it. He does it for kings, but he also does it for you and me. Isn't that glorious news?

Barbara, your battle has only begun; you have just alerted the enemy of your intention, and he'll do all he can to block it.

I firmly and fervently believe that your only hope is to stay wrapped in the Spirit of the Lord and to do what He prompts you to do and to do it quickly and decisively.

You mention that Joan has offered you a trailer to stay in. Whether you take her offer to stay in her trailer or her house or just move somewhere completely away, I believe that *you must pack your things and move out of the apartment and the environment you and your friend share*. Otherwise, Satan will insidiously drag you down and ruin you if he can.

I'm not talking about your friends; I think you know that. I'm talking about our enemy the devil that will use even our friends and family to destroy us if he can.

Consider these Scriptures, Barbara: 2 Corinthians 6:14 and 17. You're already becoming familiar with Paul's teaching about the warring that goes on continually between the flesh and the spirit. Our flesh will drag us into oblivion if we let it. This doesn't mean that the flesh is evil; it means that the devil loves to use and distort it. The beautiful thing is that once God opens our spiritual eyes and moves into our temples, we begin to see the enemy and to sense his prompting, and even though it still appeals to our flesh, we know that it will cost us our relationship with the Lord if we get into it. There is the fantastic difference. But we cannot do it without God!

I'm asking my secretary, Janet, to send you a couple of books urgently, which I think will be of great help to you. One, *Sex and the Jesus kids*, I just received from Richard Hogue, a trusted young evangelist. The other is from an older minister, Don Basham, *Face Up With a Miracle*. I think they will both help and stimulate your faith immediately.

Barbara, we are continuing to pray for you and rejoicing that God has entered your life and that you are submitting your will to His. You're heading for a very exciting life. The best thing you can do for your friends right now is move out and move on with Jesus!

Keep me posted.

Your brother,

Pat Boone

PB:jef

August 20

Dear Pat:

It doesn't seem possible that I read your book only last month on July 4th. So much has happened to me. I know I have a long way to go yet, but I'm convinced that God is taking over my life.

Tuesday evening was really difficult. My roommate broke down as she never has before. It was almost more than I could bear, but I made it through. Wednesday was a gloomy day and with the doubts from the night before, I was pretty down. I went looking for some books after my classes were over and found a couple of church supply houses. Just when I thought I wasn't going to find anything, I discovered your record "Rapture." I taped the recording so I play it in my car.

I made contact with a minister here and went to see and talk with him Saturday. The talk was good for me, but somehow I was depressed afterward.

Then Saturday night I just fell apart. But, maybe it was a good thing. My friend hadn't known until then that this decision was difficult for me and that I was having a painful time, too. It really does hurt. I know it will until I move and the wound has time to heal.

But, the most exciting thing I must tell you about is what happened today! First of all, I wasn't tremendously impressed by this minister, but he suggested I look for an apartment and I told him I would. I also indicated I would be in church today. Now this church building is an old farm house and the congregation is interracial. It's like what a Christian church was in New Testament days. I went this morning, not knowing what to expect. But I found the most wonderful group of people.

The whole service, especially communion, was deep and spiritual. The minister gave a sermon which was more like a personal talk. As the service went on, I felt so pulled, I could hardly stay in my seat. When the hymn of decision was sung, something—that burning, pulling, magnetic Something—made me respond. It's one of the most wonderful things that has ever happened to me. I rededicated my life to God's service.

Well, again that should be enough. But it isn't! I had said I would look for an apartment. After what happened last night I knew I had no other choice.

After a great number of phone calls, I found one place half way between the church and my teaching position where there were two or three one-bedroom apartments available at a reasonable rent rate. So, I went to look. They were lovely and I made an application for one. *I will probably be moving in the next two weeks.*

Choir practice meets on Tuesday evenings. I'm going this Tuesday, and I may sing this next Sunday for the service. On your album, the song "He Touched Me" seemed more than appropriate for me. I do feel as though He has touched me.

I know I'm not through all this yet, but by the grace of God and with His help, my course of action is laid. Again, I have to think of you and how I bought the *last copy* of your book—how you answered my letter. And if you hadn't I shudder to think of what might have happened. I was already thinking, *Oh, well, this is just another one of those things. It'll pass by.*

But the letter did come, and then my school chum was understanding enough to let me invade her home and take me to her church. Her minister was an exceptionally well-educated man who could lay things on the line. Then he sent me to a church near where I live which apparently has a need for me. All my school problems are working out. And then today, which I've already told you about.

Oh, I've got so much to learn and so much to do. Some of my gay friends seem to think I've "flipped" and that I'm going too fast. But, I have complete faith that whatever He wants is working out in my life as long as I say, "Here I am, do with me as you will!"

Pat, how can I ever tell you what a blessing you and your family have been to me. I love you all, dearly, and we haven't even met. But, somehow God has allowed our hearts to touch. I shared in your griefs and sorrows and the joy of your renewal to God by reading your book. Now you are sharing in mine through these letters.

When I have moved into my apartment, I'll let you know the address. As I said before I don't really expect you to write. You have so much to do! But, if you should want to and have the time, please do.

Again, God bless you and your family as you work

31

in God's infinite plan. Continue to pray for me! I'm sure your prayers have been of great help for me. *I still have the feeling that something is going to happen all the time.* So much has already happened. It's hard to believe there can be more and even more difficult to believe that there won't be. I believe that Jesus is the Christ, the Son of the Living God and He is my Savior—and with that God has my life and may do what He will.

God bless you!

Barbara

4

Lord, is there something more for me?

Dear Pat:

The move is complete as you can tell by the address. It probably was one of the most difficult things that I've ever done. I only finished yesterday.

Let me back up a little. Thank you for the books. I didn't get them from the post office until last Tuesday. Then there were two letters and the books. I don't know how, with your busy schedule, you have found time for me—but thank God for that!

Now, these last two weeks have been busy with finishing tests in regular summer school (By the way I got two *A*'s and one *B*—there's only one answer for that because I didn't really study this last part of the session) and making plans to move.

The two days between school and post-session I spent with my friend visiting her family. We, of course, had to sleep together. I told her not to worry about it. I didn't feel as close to God as I might have, but I know that He was taking care of things. Maybe this was a way of making my move easier for her. Nothing actually happened!

When we got back, things kind of fell apart, especially when she found out the apartment application had been approved. Of course, she didn't want me to go at all; but she knew if she didn't control herself, I'd leave sooner. All the while, I'm feeling a tug on me to hurry. The last couple of days were not so bad.

Now I'm out, but I'm confused. Where do I go from here? There seems to be so much I should know. At times I feel as though I'm sitting on the edge of something—it's a strange feeling. Now I have another problem.

I have been plagued since college with an ulcerous condition caused by nerves. I don't know why, but during the time I was searching for the answer for my life, I didn't have any problems, not one pain. But today for the first time I'm experiencing pain again. I thought I was ready for all that has happened. I truly want God's will in my life.

I'm having difficulty controlling my thoughts, and I try to pray and concentrate on God's will for me. I'm studying and praying—maybe not enough. Do I just wait? *Is there something else I should do*? Oh, I want so much for my life to be completely filled with God's will. Maybe I just don't know how to go about completely giving up. Could that be it?

I am so thankful that God in His infinite mercy has seen fit to release me from the bonds of my sins. I have a feeling of His presence, but I still feel as if there's something more. Maybe I'm expecting something to happen when I should wait and be patient. After all, God certainly has been patient with me.

Well, Pat, I can't really tell you much of anything else at this point. As you can tell, I'm still searching and praying for God's will to be complete in me. There are so many things I should know and I want to learn so much, but I still seem to be having difficulty. Should this be or am I still not committed?

Your letters have been a tremendous influence, and I thank God for you and your family.

Thank you for your helping hand to one who was drowning. I'm trying hard "not to let go" as you said. God bless you and your family for your continued prayers.

I must close now; I have a test tomorrow, and I haven't studied for it yet. God may be willing to help me out, but I know He's not going to do it all.

I send my deepest and warmest Christian love to you and your family. May God bless you in the work you do.

In Christian love,

Barbara

August 30

Dear Pat:

I have to tell you what has happened to me! Maybe I need to get it down on paper.

After school this morning, I had lunch and cleaned up the kitchen a little. There are many other things to do, but I wanted to study. I've already read the Hogue book which you sent. I did that yesterday before church.

But I had a miserable night last night. My stomach hurt terribly. I prayed and cried and finally went to sleep. I woke up very early this morning and asked for guidance in studying for my test, since I just couldn't study last night. The test seemed to go pretty well, at least I'm not worried.

35

Well, as I started to tell you, after last night, I wanted to study some more. So, I picked up *Face Up With a Miracle* by Don Basham. As I read, the same strange feeling came over me that I had when I first read your book and which has continued with me most of the time since. It's a sort of magnetic and vibrating feeling that I was being pulled. I don't even remember where I was in the book, but I dropped it and began to ask God for the gift of His Holy Spirit.

Oh, Pat, *something happened*! As I was praying and diligently seeking—I had to be quiet and wait—*then slowly I began to pray in a new way.* At first I thought it was me, but then the syllables started coming faster —uncontrollably fast. Tears came to my eyes and I tried to thank God in English, but I couldn't.

I may not completely understand, but I know it's real. Praise God, I *know* it's real!

I expect that I will have doubts about this later, but right now I could sing and pray and praise God all night. I have such a feeling of closeness and of the love of God. Oh, it is marvelous and His name is great among all names.

Oh, how thankful I am! How I rejoice that He was patient with me and has chosen to bring me to Him. I love Him so! All I have is His to take and use for His Kingdom.

Pat, what glory, what rapture! The song "He Touched Me" meant so much to me when I heard you sing it first. I had felt that God had "touched me." And now, I feel so close, so perfect in His love!

I don't know what I said in my prayers; but oh, Pat, I want to go on and on. I'm so full of love. God is great and merciful. It is even more glorious when I think of how depressed—to the point of being ill—I was last night and this morning. *Now I could shout and sing for the love of Christ and the presence of the Holy Spirit!*

Something tells me that we will meet and get to know each other personally. That will be a thrilling day for me. I am in tears now because there is so much love and joy in my heart.

God be with you.

Affectionately through Christ,

Barbara

September 2, 1971

Dear Barbara:

I wish you could have been at our dinner table when I read your last two letters. (I haven't been reading all your letters to the girls, of course, but I had told them about the teacher who had a serious problem and had written me for some helpful advice. And also Shirley and I have prayed together for you, without the girls really knowing all the nature of the problem.)

Janet brought your letters home from the office and handed them to me just as I was in the midst of dinner. I was too eager to wait and so I began to read them to myself. The first one, of course, described a rather "down" time; you had gone almost as far as you could go under your own steam, and really felt that there was supposed to be more. Even as I was reading your questions and your searching I was bursting to tell you that what you needed was a full measure of the Holy Spirit! I was kicking myself for not having been more specific in earlier letters.

And, then, I read your second letter; I stopped the talk at the table, gave a quick resume of your first letter, and then read your second letter out loud to the family.

As I arrived at the part in your letter where you were reading *Face Up With a Miracle* and dropped the book and began to ask God for the gift of His Holy Spirit, I'm afraid it began to get very moist and tearful around the table—certainly at my end. And before the letter was through and before we had read all of your praise to our Father that was coming irresistibly from your soul and pen, we had all been deeply touched and moved.

Isn't it incredible that God can so entwine people's lives even though they're thousands of miles apart and have never met each other? Now we can start to understand how Paul can share the joys and the sorrows of people in his own letters in the New Testament who were so far removed from where he is, and even though he might be in prison in Rome. Once Christ is in the body, there is truly a body, with the various parts becoming sensitive to the needs of the other parts. Isn't it glorious!

I'll be sending a couple more books I'd like you to read, and also just a newsier and perhaps more helpful letter; but for now I just wanted you to know of our joy and our gratitude for the way the Lord has blessed and led you.

This doesn't mean that your problems are over; and it certainly doesn't mean that Satan will not come against you with renewed vengeance; certainly he will. He's gnashing his teeth even more now that you are filled with the Spirit of Christ! But "greater is He that is in you than he that is in the world" (1 John 4:4). You and Jesus have *won* the battle—just continue to claim the victory!

Love in Jesus,

Pat Boone

PB:jef

5

valley of the shadow

September 7

Dear Pat:

I feel I must write to you again. I hope you will not become impatient with my constant writing; but at the present time, there is no one with whom I can talk concerning the reality of the Holy Spirit in my life.

I suppose Satan was not happy over the experiences which I had last week. For, last night I spent a very difficult time in the throes of temptation, doubt and guilt. I felt so alone and away from the presence of God, I would rather have been dead. Death seemed better than the pain I was suffering. All I could do was cry to God for His help!

As I had said in my previous letters, I felt so close

to something—a magnetism I couldn't describe. As I was reading Monday afternoon, I knew that God would send His Holy Spirit to speak through me. I prayed and cried in joy in some other words as I have already expressed to you. On Tuesday, the day was beautiful. I read and studied more in the evening and felt such a closeness to God which carried over to choir practice that evening. However, doubts and evil thoughts began to creep in and separate me from this feeling.

In the class I'm taking, there is a woman who has been having great difficulties. Although she has a degree in theology, her life has been plagued with problems centered mostly around an alcoholic husband. Well, Wednesday in class, I felt a particular compassion for her and prayed—but not in English! As soon as I wondered if anyone was listening, it stopped. Apparently no one had heard. But I was so shocked! *It happened right there in class!*

Wednesday afternoon and evening was probably the highlight. Of course, as I said earlier, I was beginning to doubt. I picked up *Face Up With a Miracle* and began to read again. I had the same feeling that something was going to happen. I also had a fear that the telephone was going to ring. I didn't want anything to interrupt my meditation.

My former roommate had called me two or three times with business information. I certainly didn't want to talk to her, especially now when I felt so close to God and so sure that something marvelous was happening. Well, the phone did ring! But, it was a business call about something I had ordered.

I didn't lose the feeling of closeness as I returned to the book. I finished the book and began to pray as sincerely and honestly as I knew how and again, I had the experience of speaking in something unknown to me. As I was praying the sound of the syllables changed once or twice to something that sounded like Japanese.

I sat there in a marvelous radiance which I cannot describe.

As I was sitting there, not wanting to move, I had a feeling the doorbell was going to ring. Again, I thought, *This is only my imagination.* But, it wasn't. The doorbell did ring. What more proof should I need? I went to a prayer meeting shortly after this experience Wednesday evening. The prayer time was something very special and close to God.

As Thursday and Friday came, however, I began to have my doubts. Doesn't seem possible, but I did.

I did pray for the lady in my class and was able to find a copy of your book for her. She seemed most appreciative. (By the way, your book, *A New Song,* seems difficult to find around here.)

Also, I was going on the theory that if God really had given me the gift of His Holy Spirit to direct my life, I should be able to pray for someone else and help them. Well, our minister suffers terribly with hay fever. So, I prayed fervently for him. But, this morning his hay fever was worse than ever.

But, now the really difficult part for me to talk about comes. Last night I began thinking all sorts of things about my situation. Why had I been called from a fairly contented life? What am I supposed to do? If God is truly leading me, why can't I keep control of that feeling of His presence?

Then bang! The worst of all was that *some of my old physical longings returned*—when I had thrown them away. Wow! I started crying uncontrollably and begged God's forgiveness, as I do even now.

Oh Pat, how do you know when your life is completely taken over by the will of God? I love God and want only to serve Him, yet my human nature continues to plague me with these feelings. I am so worthless. I don't see how God can put up with me or why you even try to counsel me.

41

If I can't reconcile myself to God's will, how can I possibly help others find Him? Why can I be so sure one minute that God is with me and have so many doubts and painful thoughts in the very next minute?

Pat, please pray for me that I may know the true will of our Father in Heaven for my life and that He will send the Holy Spirit to me to be my guide and power in this life. I write to you straight from my heart—revealing all those things which no man or woman knows—things which only God knows. I have no one else to talk with over these things.

I can add no more, but simply ask for your prayers.

In Christ,

Barbara

TELEGRAM

September 9

Barbara Evans

GOD WILL SEE YOU THROUGH THIS TEST-ING TIME KEEP PRAISE ON YOUR LIPS CON-TINUALLY WE ARE PRAYING WITH YOU AND A LETTER IS ON ITS WAY

Pat Boone

September 12

Dear Barbara:

After reading your letter of September 7, I felt so concerned for you that I sent you that telegram. I hope you got it and that it arrived at a time when it could help.

42

As I think back over our letters, though, I realize that when I have been concerned for you and unable to reach you "in time"—God has already been there and taken care of the situation. Really, neither of us has any cause to be anxious about anything, if we'll just trust God through those dark nights and temporary depressions. He'll *never* fail us!

Isn't it incredible that He has, by His Spirit, linked the lives of two people like us? There you are with one kind of life and environment in Hartford, and here's a busy entertainer's family in Los Angeles, and we've never met—but God has woven our lives and concerns together in prayer and study and *precious victory* by His love and His Holy Spirit! Isn't this just indescribable?

My heart went out to you when I heard you say that after that exhilarating experience of being spoken to by God's Spirit and after several days of praising Him in His language that you suddenly were assailed by doubts, temptations, fears and questions.

But Barbara, you're walking in the very footsteps of Jesus! Read from John, chapter 3, verse 13, into chapter 4. Immediately after Jesus was baptized in water and after the Spirit of God descended upon Him like a dove, and God spoke from heaven saying that He was well pleased with Jesus—*the devil tempted Him in the wilderness!*

Imagine being alone and fasting for forty days in the desert somewhere! Can you imagine the depressions, the questions, the soul-draining experience of that?

Oh, I'm sure that there were wonderful long periods where Jesus felt especially close to His Father during that wilderness fasting, but the devil knows human nature better than anybody but God. I can promise you that at the end of that forty days the devil timed things perfectly so that he could hit Jesus at His weakest possible point as far as His human nature was concerned.

Few, if any of us, would have been able to withstand him.

But Jesus, by faith and by building up His own spirit communing with His Father, was strong *spiritually* when the devil finally surfaced and began to launch his all-out assault on Jesus and His purpose for coming. *Jesus smote him with the Word of God!*

He didn't allow His feeling, His human nature, to operate or even to influence His thinking; He knew what God had said and He, in faith and spiritual surrender, just hurled these unshakeable truths at the devil until Satan had to leave Him alone. This is the pattern that we'll have to follow from now until Jesus comes!

Please don't feel badly simply because you're tempted!

Jesus was tempted with every temptation known to man! This doesn't mean that it was just laid in front of Him and that He shrugged His shoulders with no emotional feeling about it. It means that many of these wiles and tricks and traps of the devil actually *appealed* to Jesus, and I'm sure in many cases that He longed and yearned to indulge His human appetites—otherwise there would have been no temptation.

Mary Magdalene, who is known to have been one of those very closest to Jesus, is thought by scholars to have been a prostitute! She loved Jesus, and I'm quite sure that He loved her as He does us all. But there must have been many times (I'm sure the devil saw to it) when He was tempted just like Samson and Joseph and David and every man or woman who has ever lived.

It is not a sin to be tempted! Satan will never completely leave you alone; but when he comes against you as he has lately, just get out chapters 7 and 8 of Romans and read them to him *out loud*. I'm serious!

A dear friend of mine sometimes gets up in the middle of the night, when he is really being tempted, and feels himself starting to slip. He will get out his Bible and turn to many passages that flatly say that a child of God is victorious over Satan and that all the strength and authority of Jesus have been given to those people who have willingly become children of God, and he reads these things out loud to the devil. It's really a funny scene the way he describes it.

He'll pace back and forth in his living room in his pajamas with his open Bible, reading passage after passage, and saying things like,

"How do you like this, Mr. Devil?" "Try this one on, Satan!" "Have you had enough—no? Then listen to *this*!"

And on it goes until he feels that he has achieved the victory and that Satan has left him alone. As funny as it sounds, isn't this what Jesus did in Matthew 4 out there in the wilderness? I think we all need to do it.

Barbara, this is where your prayer language is so precious. In Romans 8:26-28 we have the secret weapon for all periods of depression and temptation and questioning. Whenever we can spontaneously or voluntarily pray under the direction of and in surrender to the Holy Spirit, we've got the devil on the run. Those two examples that you gave in your last letter of just spontaneously praying in the Spirit are absolutely beautiful. I know God rejoices at your growing surrender to Him—and of course, so do I.

The Apostle Paul, even late in his ministry and after all the miraculous things that God had done through Him said that he did not feel he had attained perfection (Philippians 3:12). He did not always feel himself, in your words, "completely taken over by the will of God." Read the first 10 verses of chapter 12 of 2 Corinthians for a better insight; the parallel between Paul's experience and yours I think is obvious.

Also check 2 Corinthians 2:10 and 11 for a very important clue; often we block God's blessings and strength for us by not completely forgiving those around us for something. I have no way of knowing if this is a problem for you, but I saw it as I was studying this morning and realized that most of us are not always forgiving.

Well, I better quit for now. The whole family here prays for you often (although they don't really know the problems you face), and, of course, I and they thank God with praise and love for what He has already done for you and is continuing to do. I'm sure we'll meet before too long.

Your brother in Jesus,

Pat Boone

PB:jef

6

rivers of still water

September 15

Dear Pat:

First, let me thank you for your continuing letters, especially the one dated September 12 which you wrote after reading my letter about my tremendous experience. You cannot know how deeply I need this kind of encouragement and lifting up.

I am going to try to put some thoughts down which you may or may not wish to comment on, but maybe if you see what is happening and what I'm thinking, it will help.

Sunday I made an appointment to counsel with my minister again. Although we'd had some sessions at the beginning, they didn't seem necessary for awhile; but after my session Saturday night and the way I felt when I wrote to you last, I decided to talk to him. The appointment was for Tuesday afternoon.

I felt a little better after church Sunday and writing to you. Sometimes it helps just to put things down on paper. But, even as I tried to study for my class (my test was today) I couldn't keep my mind on it. I finally decided to go back through everything, starting with your book. I'm glad I did. The book helped, again. Then I read the letters and some copies of a couple of mine. I didn't copy them all, but the one you read at the dinner table was one which I did copy.

When I finally went to bed, I felt somewhat better, but still confused.

Monday, I had plans to go over and see my former friend. There were some things she had found which she wanted me to have, and I had a couple of things for her. It was the first time I'd seen her since I moved. As I thought about it, I didn't want to go, but I felt I should.

She seemed especially well-adjusted to the situation; and although I was maybe a little upset that she adjusted so much more easily than I had expected, I came to realize that it was good. My emotions are still somewhat involved, but completely under control. I was glad after I went, because my apartment seems more like my home now. I don't belong at her place.

Tuesday I was feeling much better and I decided to take the copies of my letters to the minister. He had been reading your book, so he would know what I wanted to discuss. I really wasn't sure myself, but I knew I had to deal with the Holy Spirit.

He was sympathetic and quite willing to admit that he lacked knowledge about my prayer language. But he said he did not doubt that it could happen. I felt sure that he would accept this, although I was unsure of his reaction.

We then began to read and deal with this matter.

Pat, I think (and this is for whatever it's worth) I have been caught up in "another worldly" kind of feeling. I think I expected to be able to heal, prophesy and do all kinds of marvelous things. All of this was in a struggle to just believe for myself what had occurred. But, before I even talked to the minister, I began to realize that God doesn't want me to retreat from this world, but to live in it and do His will. If this means praising Him in other languages or healing or whatever, fine. I don't think I had accepted this. I feel now that I must say not only, "Here's my life," but "Use me *your* way."

Is it not possible that God may have other plans for me and is it necessary that I speak to Him in other languages? I really don't know; I'm only trying to find some answers.

I don't deny my experience was real, and even after Saturday night (which may have been a test) I have felt close to God with that same feeling of magnetism, but in a more realistic way.

Tonight was our prayer meeting night, again. There was a strong presence in our midst as we studied and prayed together. I can only believe it was the presence of God.

My minister felt, as do I, that it would be best not to discuss my experiences with members of the church. I'm not strong enough in the first place, and we need to do more investigating.

Pat, I sincerely do feel that my life is beginning to take shape and have purpose, but, as you said, Satan isn't too happy and my fight is only begun. I truly feel that God has "touched me" for whatever His purpose might be. I'm so thankful to Him that He was merciful to me.

There is so much I should tell you about past situations. I have an appointment with a man whom I do not want to see tomorrow; but I felt I had no choice. Did I mention the teacher whom I dated for a while about two years ago? He admittedly has no Christian beliefs.

He was asked to resign last school year—I think because of his unusual cruelty to children and inability to handle certain situations. This is only from what I observed. Why I ever saw him, I'll never know.

Well, he called me today and wants to see me. He knows about my former situation because I had no other way of getting rid of him. He's the kind that hangs on when there is no hope with a girl. He's done this with at least one other that I know. I am convinced he has great problems, but I don't think I'm strong enough to handle his and mine. I am also going to make it quite clear that there's no chance for any kind of relationship and, in fact, I'd rather not see him at all. I hope this isn't too cruel and unChristlike. I don't hold any grudge against him; I'm just afraid for my own stability in this situation.

I know that you have many people for whom you ask God's help, and I certainly don't feel that I'm so special that you must always pray for me. But, I do appreciate your prayers. And in this one area, where many young lives are involved, would you pray for me? I want so much to do God's will in all things, but with the children I especially want to do well and be a good teacher, counselor and friend. The children have always been important to me—now they're even more so.

I don't know the answer to so many things yet, Pat. But, I truly feel that God is working with me. Again, let me tell you how very dear your last letter was. I think I read it three times before I put it down. I knew I had been having some help, but a great warmth filled me when you included your family. Each time we write, I want more and more to meet you all. I'm only afraid that a few hours wouldn't be enough time to visit as much as I would like to. It would be fun just to sing with you all and talk and thank God for all He has done. Each day I seem more confident, even if I have questions or become depressed; it seems easier

to find my way back to a "rational" but loving frame
of being.

Oh, Pat, *such love fills me*, sometimes I'm without
speech. I know God has His way for me, even though
I may not know what it is.

I don't think I'll send this tomorrow. I think I'll wait
and see what occurs tomorrow afternoon, in case I should
want to write. So for tonight—may God bless the Boone
family.

Love in Christ,

Barbara

September 17

Dear Pat,

This has been another marvelous day.

I saw the teacher whom I mentioned in my previous
letter. After he had talked about his situation and I had
briefly explained my move, I approached his problem
much as a counselor would.

In the course of our conversation, I told him that
this summer I discovered something (Someone) so great
that all problems, no matter how difficult, could be
solved and/or we could have the power and wisdom to
deal with the problem. I suggested he find someone to
whom he might confide his problems—besides me—who
might help him find an inner peace. He listened but
didn't seem to really hear.

I finally told him that because I had to work out
so many things myself including doing away with the
past, I couldn't see him again. But I stressed that the
only and most important thing I could give him was
the knowledge that there is a Helper for our lives that
is greater than we ourselves.

He left very congenial, but I don't know how much

of what I said took root. There wasn't any hostility, for which I thank God.

The most wonderful thing happened this afternoon and evening. The mother of one of my students and I have been friends, and I always felt like I wanted to know her better. I had mentioned yesterday that I wanted to talk with her when she had time. She came this afternoon just to talk with me. I didn't really know how much to tell her, but I told her briefly what had happened.

She asked me a couple of questions, and I asked her if she'd like to know the whole story. She said yes, but she didn't want to pry. I told her it would be my joy to tell her. So I sat down and we began to talk. This was about 2:00 p.m. and I didn't get home until about 9:15 p.m.

Now, this family is a great family. They seem very close to God. They all participate in church work, and the parents are trying to raise the children with a good set of Christian standards.

I think I may have been able to help her a little— only because of God's leading me by His Holy Spirit. I do know that we hugged each other two or three times tonight because of God's love.

(Note: As we hugged each other, there were no other feelings or thoughts other than Christian love and comfort—isn't it marvelous?)

As you can see, there are some channels of opportunity opening up to me which I never dreamed possible. What is so incredible is that I never could have talked to these people the way I have without some other help— the presence of God in my life.

Today, more than ever, I am so thankful to God for being merciful to me and snatching me away from a doomed life.

Again, I send love to you and your family. You can see that things are smoothing out. I have put my complete trust in God's will for my life. How wonderfully

He sustains us. I do praise His name for all these blessings and today especially the blessing of the Boone family in my life.

You know, my former roommate couldn't see how I would survive without someone to love me. I've always needed a great deal of love. But I'll tell you this—*there is nothing to compare to this love*. Oh, glorious and wonderful God who has blessed me with His love!

Oh, Pat, how I love my God and how much love I feel for others in serving Him. It fills me up.

In Christ,

Barbara

September 19

Dear Pat:

Oh, Pat, there's no way I can humanly tell you what an exciting day today has been.

I had a call from my minister before I left the apartment and he asked me to sing again this Sunday since our choir director had been out of town.

I decided to sing "I Asked the Lord." You know, the one I did on the tape I sent you. When I sang—I know God was using me! In the car going to church I had tried to sing, but I felt like I was catching cold; my voice wasn't steady. I asked for God's help to praise and glorify His name. And Pat, *it came out*. But what was more wonderful was the feeling that God was using me like an electric current to reach the people.

Each Sunday the church service—especially communion—becomes more precious, and I don't know how that's possible.

This afternoon—on the spur of the moment(?)—I called a friend to see if she would come over and see my apartment and try on some dresses which I couldn't wear. Well, she suggested I might come to her church to sing. But Pat, that's not all I did, and this is something I could never have done on my own. I gave a personal witness to these people. Oh, I hope I'm not going too fast. But God worked through my voice again. He's making it impossible for me to turn around and go back. Isn't that great? How I love Him—how I thank Him for His mercy to me.

Pat, *I really think I'm going to be all right now.* God is faithful to me. I have had some bad moments and continuing evil thoughts. But I constantly lay these problems at my Savior's feet, ask His help to overcome them, and offer my life for His service. Oh, my Lord and my God, how I do love and adore thee.

You were right—marvelous things are happening. It's absolutely unbelievable, but I will not turn around. Satan will be defeated! God will be victorious!

Rejoice with me, all you in the Boone family. I love you and thank God for your friendship and prayers. May God continue to bless your lives. Someday, sometime, we will meet and you all will know how deeply I love you because of God's great and miraculous love for me.

Pat, I have not worshipped God in a prayer language since I last wrote of doing so, but I could never doubt God's faithfulness to me and the presence of the Holy Spirit working in His own miraculous way. This room, my heart, my life, my whole being are at this moment filled with the very presence of God! Jesus is truly my great and wonderful King, Lord and Master of all life.

I could go on and on, but I had better close. Tomorrow is the beginning of the school year with the children. Continue to pray for me that I might be an effective witness to my students. Don't be afraid to tell me if you think I'm going too fast. Things have never happened to me like this before, so I don't know. I have so much to share and such a desire to share it. I'm afraid I might be too bold. But I love my Lord and I want others to krow His tremendous love for them, also.

As I say, I'll close for now. All I can say is "God bless you all!" We shall meet someday, either here on this earth or in God's Kingdom of glory. I send my love—through Christ, my Lord.

P.S. I love you!

12:15 a.m.

Pat—

I thought I was through, but I had to open the envelope and add this after what just happened in the last half-hour.

I have been so much in the presence of God tonight. I wasn't sleepy, so I decided to read in my Living New Testament. I had your family album on softly as I was reading. When "Sweet, Sweet Spirit" came on, I *had* to turn off all the lights. I just sat for a few seconds and felt the presence of God, then His presence was so overpowering, I turned off the tape and I had no choice but to kneel in His presence even though I'm quite alone (in body only).

Oh, Pat, what a great and wonderful peace fills me! *God allowed me to praise Him in my prayer language, again.* I just let go, let my love flow to God even as His love flows to me. I am completely His and "He is at work in me, helping me want to obey Him, and then helping me do what He wants." *You told me that once in your very first letter.* Oh, and it's true!

What more can happen? I have no comprehension, but God is my guide in all things—I love Him!

Again, I say—

Love in Christ,

Barbara

55

7

song of joy

September 22

Dear Pat:

I was unable to mail this today, and I'm glad, for your letter came.

Although you are right—God is taking care of the situation—I still appreciate and need your encouragement. He is leading in my life. When I talk with other people, I can feel His presence in, around, and through me.

I have been reading, and the passages of Scripture which you suggested to me have helped me in understanding. I think I'm going to memorize some and carry them in my heart.

Yes, I do find it incredible that God has linked our lives! There are so many things, as you will know by

57

this letter, that are fantastically unbelievable and yet true! My life is changed; and although I talk to some of my old friends on the phone, I have no desire to see them. Maybe it's because I fear temptation. But desiring not to see them is a tremendous change on its own. Of course, there are many other differences, too.

Pat, the Scripture which was especially meaningful to me was that in 2 Corinthians. I do feel I am weak in many ways and only through the power of God's love and Holy Spirit am I sustained. If I must bear this weakness, so that I will continually call upon my Lord, then I will be happy to do so—wanting only God's will in my life.

You also mentioned that God's blessings and strength might be blocked by not forgiving those around us. I've been praying that God will help me forgive those who have hurt me in the past. I really feel that He has given me forgiveness, *especially for my father.* However, I still have difficulty in feeling the love for him I think God wants me to have. I'm praying that God will fill me with His love.

It may help you to understand my problem in this area of my life if I write out the things that have happened in the past. I've been wanting to let you know more anyway, but I have not been sure about how to put it down. I know my life has changed, but others can't really understand because they don't know all the past.

To God be all the glory for the change He's brought in my life, for the faithful way He sustains me and for the miraculous way in which He uses me!

Again, there are not words to tell you, Pat, how I appreciate your letters at a time when my faith is made stronger. I can only thank God and pray that He will continue to bless the Boone family for whom I have such love as He has given me.

Your sister in Christ,

Barbara

Hi, Little Sister!

A most wonderful thing just happened! I was on my way down to a recording session—recording a hymn album—and I put the cassette you had sent me into my car player for the first time. I had assumed that it was a speaking letter and had no idea that you were singing on it—or that you would be singing *some of the very songs I was recording,* including "Nearer My God To Thee!"

You can imagine the joy I felt as I heard you praise the Lord so beautifully! Before long—I was singing along with you and arrived at the recording studio with just the right spirit to go in and record some of those songs in a true spirit of praise and thanksgiving to the God who sees us and hears us and knows us and loves us so deeply.

Of course, I'll keep the cassette in the car, and you and I will be doing some duets from time to time in mutual praise to our God. I don't know if that idea had occurred to you when you sent the songs, but since it happened so naturally, I'll just make it a regular thing. Your singing is really lovely, and it's obvious you know more about music from a technical standpoint than I do. The Lord may be planning to give me some voice lessons—through you! And I'm not kidding!

Paul says in Ephesians 5:19 and 20 that we *should* be speaking to each other in "psalms and hymns and spiritual songs, singing and making melody in our hearts to the Lord, always giving thanks for all things in the name of our Lord Jesus Christ to God, even the Father." How incredible that He made it possible for two strangers to have this joy first through my album and then by way of your cassette! I certainly intend to send you the first copy of the hymn album!

Keep the faith, Barbara, and as Paul admonished

Timothy, continually "kindle afresh the gift of God which
is in you." (2 Timothy 1:6)

Your brother in Jesus,

Pat

PB:jef

8

struggles without, fears within

Surprise! I can type. After trying to read what I had written, I decided that even my horrible typing was better than my undecipherable handwriting. So here it is:

Dear Pat,

Tonight I am thanking God for His many blessings.

Something upsetting happened to me. I found an obscene note, typewritten, in my lesson plan book. At first I thought it was just a piece of scrap paper. Sometime after a class Wednesday afternoon and class at the same time on Thursday the message was inserted. I was shocked when I realized what it was. But then I said a quick prayer and felt sorry for the person who wrote it. Four years ago something similar happened

61

and I went to pieces. What a difference! Only to God can the credit be given for my reaction in this case (and all others, lately).

I started reading *The Cross and the Switchblade* Wednesday. I can see why you became so excited about reading it. Some time ago I saw the movie, but that was before the change in my life. It had an impact upon me even then, but parts of the book hit me even harder now, especially the parts where people like my old self were involved.

Well, I had just finished the book Friday evening when the phone rang. A man introduced himself and said he was my neighbor. He asked me to come over; he said he was sitting there with a scotch and water and needed someone to talk to.

Of course, I said no. He offered to visit me instead and again I said no. He asked why not, and I replied because I would most likely be praying.

This started a long conversation on "religion." He said he was agnostic if not atheistic. I told him that God still loved him. All during the conversation, he tried to persuade me to come to his apartment. I kept saying no.

Then he began to call me a phoney—said I didn't know anything about the problems of the world—Vietnam, drugs, sex, and politics.

I told him I wasn't any more innocent of sin than anyone else. He said, "Like what?" I told him that was something I was only obliged to confess to God. He hung up.

Then I called a friend, and while I was talking on the phone, the doorbell rang. It was the fellow who had called earlier.

I saw him through my door-peep and he looked drunk. Persistently he asked if he could come in, and I said no. I told him that I was on the phone.

He called me a phoney again and said I didn't know what it was all about. I told him that I knew God's love was great enough to reach him just as it had reached me. He kept on talking, and then I told him that he'd better go or I would have to call our building manager. He left.

The most important part of this is that I tried to turn the problem over to God—I asked for His guidance to say the right thing to this young man and not to have fear.

Maybe the fellow was right. Maybe I am phoney not to face him. But, in his condition, I didn't think I'd accomplish anything in person except place myself in a vulnerable position. The man did say he worked with young people who had problems with things such as drugs, sex, and alcohol. He said that he tried to get them to see the need for "human" values. What I couldn't make him understand was there are no values without God.

Pat, I'm still having problems with my thoughts, but they are becoming boring, and God is filling my life with so much more.

Today I went to visit my former friend. The last time I went, I was sort of upset. This time, I was relaxed and felt God had me and the situation in hand. She asked me if I was happy, and I could honestly say, "Yes, very!" But the miraculous thing is—within less than a month my feelings for her have completely changed. She is *only* a friend. Isn't that great!

I have confidence in my Savior, and your encouragement has been a great help toward gaining that confidence. I must close for tonight; I'll write again, later.

Much love in Christ,

Barbara

October 1

Dear Pat,

I am confused about some things. However, I praise

63

God that I now have confidence that He will show me the way! It is so wonderful to *know* that!

Saturday, I went over to my former friend's house. I think she realizes that one of these days we probably won't even see each other. I only go now because she's lonely and we do have much in common, both being teachers. But, Pat, I was truly glad to get back home.

Sunday was another marvelous day! The fellowship of my church and the tremendous power of communion with God fills my heart to overflowing. The message was on the subject of "A Personal Encounter with Christ." I lived the last few glorious weeks of my life over in a few short minutes. I cried for joy at God's matchless love and mercy to me.

In our church bulletin Sunday was a notice that our minister was to speak for final vespers at family camp, which was being held at the same camp which I attended as a teenager when I was so close to God. I went along. Oh, Pat, it was tremendous! I knew I was going all day Sunday, and I was so thrilled and rejoicing. I prayed to God many times thanking Him for His love: finally, I could say no more and God allowed the Holy Spirit to take over. This happened in church, driving the car and even while at the camp vesper service. I prayed quietly in the prayer language God has given to me.

But then I went over to visit a friend whose husband is a retired Baptist minister. He has had a great deal of experience counseling young people, and I thought he might be able to help me. He listened to my story and here are a couple of things which I am confused about.

He said that when a person accepts Christ and is baptized, believing in Him, that he is saved. Even if he turns away from God after he has once believed, God cannot deny him. His rewards will not be as great, but he will be saved. Do you have anything to say on this subject?

The other matter is concerning my prayer language. He said that the Word of God speaks plainly that where those speak in other languages, someone *must* interpret for edification. He asked me if I understood what I spoke. Of course, I did not and do not. *However, I know these experiences are real.* He seemed very sure that it was absolutely necessary that someone should interpret. He did say, however, that giving my life over to God was the most important thing.

Now, Pat—I don't know whether this matters or not—I felt God's presence with me while I was in this home, but I felt a very strong gap between myself and these people. I had expected to feel the closeness I've felt with others when sharing this experience and change in my life. But tonight when I left, I didn't even feel the close friendship I've always felt. I didn't feel animosity—I just felt distance. I hope you can understand what I'm trying to explain.

The minister also said something about an "emotional experience." Of course, it *has* been emotional, but it has also been peaceful. The other night I went to sleep praying. I am closer to God and feel His presence with me constantly. It is more and more easy to allow the Holy Spirit to speak through me.

Am I wrong?

In Christ,

Barbara

October 4

Dear Sister:

This will have to be a short one, but I want to share with you 1 John 4:15-17. The last part of the 17th verse jumped out at me last week—"because as he is, *so also are we in this world.*" Isn't that fabulous?

65

Hang on! We love you and pray for you, and know He's with you and will sustain you! Just keep praising Him!

Your brother,

Pat

PB:jef

October 6

Brother Pat!

Talk about joy—your letter of Sept. 25 thrilled me! Thank God for our friendship!

I'm so happy that my tape did what I intended. I wanted to share in song with you as you have shared with me. I have been singing duets and obligato parts for the songs on your recordings almost every day. Really, I've almost worn my tapes out, but I have the records! I am continuing to sing as much as I can.

In some ways, I'm finding it hard to continue my teaching. I want to talk to people and sing and work for the Lord every minute. Teaching little children's songs sometimes becomes a strain. I want to stop and say, "Oh, children, if I could only tell you how much God loves you!" And yet I know that God will work through me even in my teaching if I ask His guidance.

The following weekend will be a very special one (they all are, now); but this one more so. I will be returning to Darian to visit Joan and her family and sing in her church where must of my story began to fall into place. My most troubled time and the time of my complete conviction and decision came in a field on her farm. I want to go back, and how I shall rejoice!

May God continue to pour out His richest blessings upon the Boone clan! I love you all.

Your Sister in Christ,

Barbara

October 12

Dear Barbara:

I'm dictating this as we drive to the airport to begin our tour. It's actually an important letter for several reasons, so I hate to hurry but I must.

Don't let anyone—your friend, a minister, or *any-one*—*rob you of the experience you had and are continuing to have with your prayer language.*

When the apostle Paul talked about interpreting he was speaking to the Corinthians about their worship services *as a group.* In the first two or three verses of the 14th chapter of 1 Corinthians he talks about praying privately and how it is unfruitful to his mind, but that his spirit is edified. This is a personal thing, and it is your own communication with the Lord.

Naturally, if you were to be in a group of believers it would be disconcerting and out of order to just continue to pray out loud in your prayer language without anyone to interpret for the edification of the group. But when you're praying and praising privately it's a different matter. Do you see it? Don't let anybody rob you of this joy.

You are literally the bride of Christ! He has drawn you lovingly into a new world of spiritual desire and eternal love with Him. He wants you to *possess* this kingdom, like a trusting child and the new creature that you are.

Paul says that his language of love is to build you

up spiritually as you speak to Him privately; but that in a group worship, under proper circumstances, the Holy Spirit may speak through you to bless the whole group. Always be sensitive to that second possibility; but meanwhile, like Paul, speak your love, joy and surrender intimately to Jesus in heavenly mysteries.

And do it often.

I hope that your other friend is right about "once saved, always saved." However, Matthew 5:29 indicates something different to me, from Jesus' own lips. But, my understanding is limited, and I can only hope that she is right. So many Scriptures indicate that it is possible to "fall away" or as Paul said, "after I have preached to others, I myself should be disqualified." (1 Corinthians 9:27) However, as long as you or anyone else is trying to serve God, I know that He makes up for our inadequacies and our weaknesses—through Christ.

I've asked Janet to send you a copy of your first letter to me, and a copy of one of the recent ones. It moves me deeply to see the incredible difference between the two. The change in you is so obvious that I think you will be thrilled to relive it just a little.

And now, I have something for you to ponder: if we completely shield you, both name and city and in every other way—do you feel as I do that the chronicle of our correspondence could be put into a small book form for the benefit of others who feel that they are trapped in hopeless situations? I really think that the Holy Spirit has written another living epistle through our letters. Of course, we can change or delete anything that would pinpoint a place or specific people. I'm just so anxious to share with others what God has done for you.

How do you feel about it?

Please feel under no pressure about this. If you have the least reluctance we'll abandon it immediately. Our relationship has become too precious for me to strain it or make either of us self-conscious. I just believe, as I look back over a three-month correspondence that anybody in his or her right mind would be thrilled to look over our shoulders and to benefit from the startling example of God's mercy and power and immediacy.

God bless and protect you.

Your brother in Christ,

Pat Boone

PB:jef

October 15

Dear Sister:

Since we have begun to correspond the Lord has made me very sensitive to the enormity of the problem you have had. I've been involved in a lengthy interview for X magazine with a man who is a homosexual—who's trying to write an objective article about the Jesus Movement! Also, friends of ours have been sharing their faith in Christ with a young couple. The husband is a former minister who lost his congregation when he began to molest some of the small boys in his congregation. From there he has become a complete degenerate—swapping sons with another man and finally corrupting *his own son.* Our friends believe that the Lord has put them in contact with this couple as a test case.

"If God can rescue and rehabilitate this man, then there is no such thing as 'impossible,' " he says.

These incidents simply dramatize the urgent need to let people know that Jesus loves everybody and supplies the answers that they need, whatever they are.

I wanted you to know that we sympathize with you in the struggle you are having, but also *rejoice* with you in the victories God is giving.

I hope that these are days of great rejoicing for you as you examine the path along which you've traveled and see the Lord's hand on you from the very beginning.

The Boones rejoice with you and send our love. Please be in touch whenever you can.

Your brother in Jesus,

Pat Boone

PB:jef
Enclosure

9

God moves in

Dear Pat,

I have so much to tell you and ask you, I don't know where to begin. My joy in the Lord is so great, I can't begin to emphasize its depth in writing! When I think I'm so full nothing else can happen, something else *does* happen.

While I was visiting at Joan's, I had a terrible cold. This is something that I have been plagued with since I was young, especially during my teenage years. All the time I was visiting, I took medication prescribed by the doctor and the vitamins I always took. Yet God gave me my voice so I could sing for church even with the cold.

Then last night, while I was praying, I suddenly felt as if God would cure my cold. While I was still in the attitude of prayer, I put all my medicine in the garbage disposal. Today my cold is all but gone! I know that God has cured me. This is tremendous because I always have the kind of colds that put me to bed for several days. Praise the Lord for His healing hand!

My stomach problems have disappeared, too. No one can know how painful those stomach cramps are unless they have had them. At times there's nothing you can do but ache. God has the cure for both our physical and spiritual needs!

My life is so completely changed, Pat. To God be the glory and honor forever!

Now, Pat, I've just found out that you are going to be in New Haven. Would there be any possibility of seeing you while you're here? I don't know exactly how to proceed on this, but I'll be at the show. If you could have your secretary write or even call and give me some details, I would surely appreciate getting to meet you and your family.

May God bless and protect the Boone family as they travel and serve the Lord. My prayers and my love go with you.

In Christian Love,

Barbara

October 26

Dear Pat,

Although I hope and trust in the Lord that I will see you Saturday, I had to write tonight.

There is one development which I'd like to tell you about. I've been trying to get away from even seeing my former roommate and old friends. Yet I have felt an obligation to talk to her when she calls and asks me over. I have been thinking I might be able to help her. But this weekend I feel as if a door is closing.

I'm sure now that she has been trying to work up courage to ask me some questions. I told her a little of my plans. I also told her that I was happier than I had ever been and that I would rather die than give up what I have found. I tried to be specific, but she continually cut me off—at least I didn't feel like I could say anything more.

I mentioned that I might go away during Christmas vacation. We have spent every Christmas vacation together for the last several years. Before I moved, she had mentioned going to Florida this Christmas. I'm sure that she still hoped I might go, but my new ideas put a halt to that. Pat, I just couldn't spend Christmas vacation or any other vacation with her even if I just stay right here in my apartment.

Well, she said we didn't have anything but school in common now. Thank God—she's right!

Pat, *I just cannot comprehend how tremendously God has dealt with me!* Reading my first letter to you the other evening was like reading a page of ancient history. I could not even *remember* the emotions I felt for my friend at the time I wrote. Then seeing the other letter— Thank you, God—Oh, *thank you!*

I had the most marvelous and personal prayer session with God on my way to choir practice tonight. Your letter and the whole change—how incredible—in my life struck me full force, and I prayed as I never have before in my prayer language to our wonderful and glorious God.

Thank you for the answers to some of my questions. As far as my prayer language is concerned, I didn't have much to do with that. When the Spirit moves, I hope I allow Him to work in and through me.

As far as the "once saved, always saved" doctrine, I have read the book of Hebrews which was recommended—

73

and falling away is warned against. One passage of Scripture comes to my mind, but I can't recall where it is found. The context is that once you have the Spirit if you turn away and deny Him, you can never come again. It's something like that.[1] See why I have to go to Bible college? I need to know so much and I want to learn as much as I can about God. I want to know and do His will in my life.

One of my biggest concerns now is my family. I was able to tell them about the change in my life. But I'm still having difficulty loving them like I feel I should. I get up-tight around them. However, I know that God is able to break down this barrier.

I continue to praise God for all His blessings, and tonight I thank Him for the way He will make Himself felt at your programs. He is great and He is love!

God be with you and yours.

Your sister in Christ,

Barbara

November 7

My Dearest Sister and Brother in Christ,

I have many things. First, I cannot begin to thank the Lord and you for allowing me to visit with you and your daughters. Pat said I received a "spiritual smorgasbord," and he certainly was right.

Other than our prayer time together, one of the most precious times for me was talking to you, Shirley. I didn't know how you would feel about me, and I was apprehensive, to say the least, about talking to you. But praise the Lord—I did, and what a joy and uplift I found! Of course, Pat's letters have been my greatest source

---

[1] Heb. 6:4-6

of encouragement in the past; but talking to you opened wide the door for complete friendship, love and fellowship with the whole Boone family.

Several people who knew about my meeting with you in person were worried that I might put Pat in a place of worship or that I might have a teenage-style crush on him. Well, I was in awe about the whole situation, but praise the Lord, my only love for him and the whole family is in Jesus. Maybe you had some of the same apprehensions. I don't know. But I love you both so much—I had to share this with you.

After you two left Monday night, I had such a peace and joy in the Lord. For the first time when I got ready for bed and began to pray again I *sang* in my prayer language. It was so beautiful. I have wanted to do this since I read it in your book. God is so precious!

When I got back to Hartford, I stopped to tell my minister and his wife about my visit with the Boones. He asked me if I thought it would help him to hear me pray in my prayer language. I told him I didn't know; I didn't even know if I could. It is not something you turn off and on like a radio.

Well, we did have prayer together, and I was allowed to pray—first in a whisper—then aloud. I didn't really know what they thought, but I felt a strong sense of the presence of God. Of course, I had felt Him near anyway—I had prayed almost all the way from New Haven to Hartford. And what a beautiful sunset the Lord provided that afternoon! I drove right into it and felt as though I could have gone right straight into the arms of my loving Savior.

And now dear people, I must close for now. I have much school work to do. I continue to pray for you and your work. God be with you and peace in Christ our Savior.

Deepest affection in Christ,

Barbara

75

Dear Barbara:

I had a couple of letters from you when I returned, and although I'm not looking at them at this moment, I wanted to write you a note of assurance and encouragement.

I know that you will go through many lonely days and nights and valley experiences between the mountain top highs. We all do. My keenest thought as I read your letters was that you have just come out of a ten-year period of virtual surrender to Satan, although, of course, you didn't realize it or look at it that way. Still you had faith in your manner of life, and believed that if you kept on that the good times and the happy times would return.

Although I'm confident that the Lord will not subject you to ten years of misery, I do know already from my own experience that our faith is tested time and again through periods of loneliness and seeming defeat.

But the Lord does tell us we will never be tempted beyond that which we are able to bear, and that *Jesus Himself learned obedience through the things that He suffered.* The glorious news is that after each period of loneliness and testing (which can be shortened by our praise of God and our continued confession of our dependence upon the living Jehovah), He gives us new insights and deeper faith and renewed strength.

So instead of continual and gradual descent into the depths with Satan, it is a gradual and progressive and increasingly exhilarating climb toward heaven with the Living God!

Even in your last letter the Lord was renewing your strength and giving you the insight you need to begin to go back through your childhood and former associations and review even within yourself what the Lord has done for you.

I do believe that as you retrace some of the steps

of your childhood and family life and then get specific about the events and associations of tragedies as well as the seemingly happy involvements of the last ten years, that your faith will soar to new heights and your gratitude and devotion will increase immeasurably. I hope you will write it down. I'll look forward to reading it. And I believe the Lord will bless you even as you undertake this assignment. A lot of times we don't really appreciate where we are until we look at where we've been. It's like the old farmer who said, "I may not be what I *oughta* be, but thank God I ain't what I *used* to be!"

Through reading the lives of David, Noah, Cain, Abel, and Solomon, we can see that these people in the Bible weren't "hot house plants"—they were really human beings with passions and pride and the possibility of all kinds of human error. The glory comes when we see how God elevated people like Paul and David and Noah and Rahab above their sinful natures into something supernaturally beautiful.

God bless you, Barbara; we pray for you all the time.

Your brother,

Pat Boone

PB:jef

10

autobiography: descent into darkness

November 13

Dear Pat,

I appreciate your suggestion that I attempt to recount the story of my life. Some of the things may not seem as significant as others, but they have come out as I have been counseling with my minister. It's really been hard to sit down and write all this out, but I have to get what happened into the open. I want to be free from all the feelings of my past. I want God's love to flow through me to others. Praise the Lord!

I was born in a city hospital while my father was in the service during World War II. After the war, we moved from the city to a farming community.

When I was about eight, tragedy struck our family. A child was lost at birth, and my parents, especially my father, grieved heavily over the loss of this child. Later I found that this experience drew my mother toward God, but my father became very bitter.

A year or so after the baby's death my parents had another child, a son.

Shortly after my brother was born, I first began examining the human body. Some other girls and I played a game called "hospital," and we did a lot of exploring. This may have been the beginning of my guilt feelings about sex.

About this same time, I had a very bad scare. I went to the grocery store one day for my mother. On the way back, a man stopped me on the bridge, which I had to cross to get home, and asked me if I'd like to see something. Since it was near Easter, I thought he had a rabbit or an animal; but then he asked me to go under the bridge. I said "no" and started to run home as fast as I could. He chased me on foot for a while, and then he got into his car. Fortunately, I got home before he got too close. But the experience scared me and my whole family and made us more cautious.

While my brother was still very young my parents discovered he had a controllable but incurable illness. At this point he became very important in their lives.

My father was again distraught. As a result, my brother was continually "babied." I probably developed mixed emotions of jealousy and guilt because my brother couldn't help the fact that he was sick. I have also felt indirectly responsible for his illness, because I had taken care of him when he was very little and may not have watched him as carefully as I should.

When I was in the sixth grade, I started going to church. Although my family did not seem a bit interested in going themselves, they apparently didn't have too much objection to my going—at first.

Church meant a great deal to me. I liked the people and was touched by the sermons and Sunday school lessons about the love of Jesus. I wanted to be baptized, but my father said no, and my mother agreed. I think this was the beginning of the difficulties I was to have with my father.

Finally, after much discussion and persistence, my parents agreed, and I was baptized. It was one of the most beautiful days of my life.

I was really very happy in the church. I learned about Jesus and did well in Sunday school. But my family, especially my father, resented my absence from family activities on Sunday. Sometimes I had to beg for permission to go to church. Other times I went and made arrangements to spend the day with one of the church families. I grew to love many of the people there.

As I entered Junior High School I became more involved in outside activities, especially singing. One of my girl friends at church and I did a lot of singing together. I liked to do solos, as well, and sang in the church choir.

My mother and I became a lot closer at this time. And as we grew closer, my father appeared jealous of our closeness. At the same time his resentment toward my participation in church functions began to increase. Things got so difficult at times that I used to dream about how to commit suicide. I always thought cutting my wrists would be the best way.

High school became very special to me because we had a new, full-time music teacher. Since I was interested in music, I was very excited.

During my high school years, I became very fond of this music teacher because she would listen to my family problems. She would take time to talk with me when she saw that I was terribly upset. Many days I would go to school and get sick shortly after I arrived. I'm sure this was a nervous condition and probably the beginning of the stomach problems which developed later. My teacher always came to see me during these spells of illness and I liked her a lot.

Since I did have a lead voice, I sang a great deal at church and school. Thus I developed an overwhelming attachment to music and my music teacher. I remember a note which I wrote once, telling a friend that I didn't know why but I felt so funny—"all gooey"—around my teacher. I think I even said I loved her.

I became more active in church and school activities, especially those involving music. The disagreements at home over church activities entered into other issues as well. I didn't help around the house as I should have, and my father was constantly scolding me about this.

One incident which occurred at this time made life difficult for me. The only one who understood my problem was my music teacher. She believed me, but even she found the situation incredible. What happened was that the principal of the high school made an overt pass at me when I went to his office to ask him about a math problem. He touched me in inappropriate places; I was badly shaken up because of his forwardness. I told my best girl friend. I was called in, eventually, by two of the women teachers and questioned. They thought that the principal was just being fatherly, but I knew better. I certainly stayed away from him as much as possible after that.

When I was about sixteen, a young man whom I had known and liked since I was twelve called to ask me for a date. He was then twenty-two and had just returned from the service. We attended the same church, so this was a fine arrangement and my parents even approved of him.

But one Sunday he didn't pick me up for church as he had promised, so I rode the church bus there instead. I thought maybe he had had car trouble again. When

I got there I saw that he was already at church, seated with another girl *who turned out to be his wife.*

I hadn't known he was married. I was very fond of him (maybe too much), and this nearly broke my heart. I think that was the beginning of the end of my dating boys.

Afterwards I rode the church bus to my grandmother's house where my parents were. They knew right away that something was wrong. That day I wrote one of my first love poems.

I turned more and more to my music teacher for encouragement and advice on my home situation. She didn't always think my persecution at home was as bad as I made it out to be. Maybe it wasn't, but it enabled me to gain her attention. I was always buying her little gifts. I even wrote a short prosaic thing called "Fire of My Heart!"

> When love's last embers race across my heart's blank page as the dying fire of a mighty forest, my soul shall stand bare against the cold winter of loneliness. The shattering pain of undying devotion shall cease, and in its place will come a hollow, deft feeling of complete emptiness. In the dim years to come, nothing will be left to own but a living memory of those full and glorious days I once knew.
>
> And now, my heart, the raging flame has cooled its race and is desperately vying with its own death. Remember the solemn moments, the joyous hours, the marvelous days, the peaceful weeks, the exciting months and the memory-laden years. Hold on to just this one undying coal and watch the never-ending glow of the love that once was the fire of my heart.

From this friendship there grew an unusual sort of attachment. My heart would pound whenever she would drive by in her car, and it would sink if I didn't see her. But I didn't understand this situation. I only knew that at times I was miserable. I prayed for God to let my love be returned. Many days I would come home from school so lonely that I would go to the bedroom and cry for hours. Sometimes I would cry myself to sleep. No one ever came and asked what was wrong with me; they just let me cry.

During my Junior year, probably after my disappointment with my twenty-two-year-old boyfriend, I changed my membership in the community church to a denominational church. I only mention this because it seems to me now as a significant step away from God. I was seeking more of the social aspects of church *rather than the spiritual.* Before this I had planned to go to Bible College when I graduated from high school. Even as I continued to think about this, I was drawn more to music school.

My senior year was terrific, and yet sad. I knew that when school was out I probably would not see my music teacher very often, if at all. I sang that year more than ever, not publicly, just in the music room to my teacher. By this time I knew how to sing passionate love songs. I would stand behind the piano and sing with all my heart while she played. I longed for something to be said, but it never was.

After graduation, which was both exciting and sad, my summer worked out so that I could be near my friend. We saw each other almost every day. She gave me a couple of books to read that opened my eyes completely to the possibilities of "gay life." From that point, nothing stopped me. With each visit, I tried desperately to convince her that this was what I wanted.

If the story were not so sad, it would be beautiful. You know—just the right things were said one day, one of the songs which I had continually sung to her was playing on the radio—and then we kissed.

I thought I would explode. All the longings of the past few years seemed to be lost in that kiss. And yet, there seemed to be a desire for more than this. My life had opened to a new world, and I could not rest until I possessed it.

I can't explain why this all came about. Maybe it was because of my struggles with my father; maybe it was my disappointment in my dating life; or maybe it was just because I asked for it, and God let me have what I thought I wanted. But this was only the beginning. There was much pain and heartache yet to come.

In the fall, I went away to college. The day I left was another sad and lonely event in my life. My friend had told me that she should stop seeing me and had encouraged me to date fellows.

But during Christmas vacation she called when I was home to invite me to my first gay party. That night we were "married." By this, I mean we stayed in a motel all night, and for the first time I learned how to make love physically.

We saw each other as often as possible during the second semester of my freshman year of college. In spite of all this, I made decent grades, but I hated the school. I suppose that was because it was too far away from my lover. So, at the end of the year, I transferred to a school closer to my friend's apartment—it was to be our apartment. That next summer I spent there loving and being loved.

During the year following, I met other gay people. Most of them were business or professional people. We had a small group of friends and sometimes we went to the gay bars, but we were the quiet ones no one would ever suspect of being so unconventional.

I can't remember exactly when in the sequence of events, but ultimately my friend and I had some difficulties which we could not seem to work out. We couldn't seem to stay apart, and we couldn't seem to stay together. It was torture.

I remember many nights and days when I would cry for hours because I was so lonely and wanted to be loved. I thought that I would rather be dead than go through the pain and agony that I felt.

During this period I renewed acquaintance with a softball player I had met at one of the gay bars. I fought against the possibility of anything happening between us, physically. The one night we did spend together made me ill. I was used to gentleness; she was rough. Although we saw each other on and off for a while I could not submit to her again.

These experiences caused me to stay alone most of the time. However, I visited my friend at every opportunity and still longed to be with her.

During these visits, our gay friends suggested that we live together as roommates for financial reasons. My friend agreed after much prompting; and as we began to share the same dwelling place, we became closer as friends than we had ever been as lovers.

Christmas, a year later, my friend had completely surrendered the separation between us. All of the old barriers about age difference were gone, and we were "married" again. After the ins and outs of the past seven or eight years, years of struggling and loneliness, I believed that God had finally answered my prayers. We still had problems, but they were the same kind that most married couples have, even normally married ones.

We didn't go out much except to visit close friends, and we rarely entertained. Both of us were very busy in our jobs and we shared in a great deal of each other's work.

I had been to several churches in the past few years, but I had not seriously considered the full commitment of membership to any of them. I was perfectly content now to live my day-to-day life with the one I had always loved so dearly.

A year went by and our anniversary Christmas was full of love. We were both happy.

I must add that although we seemed happy, there were times when I had physical desires which would go untended for several months. During these times I learned how to successfully excite myself by physical manipulation (masturbation). When there was a "dry spell," I would take care of myself. To my knowledge, my lover never knew this. So, we were happy and I was satisfied—or was I?

Then through a movie magazine article, I learned of your book, *A New Song*. You had been a favorite of mine during my high school days. I watched your movies and enjoyed hearing you sing. I had bought your book for teenagers, *Twixt Twelve and Twenty*. But I had not heard much about you in the past few years and did not know that you and Shirley had had difficulties or anything about this new life. But I couldn't find your new book right away, so I forgot about it.

One day when I was picking up a book which had been ordered at one of the bookstores near campus I spotted a copy of *A New Song*. I can't explain my reactions when I saw it, but I felt like the book had my name on it before I even picked up a copy to buy.

You know the story from this point.

Tonight I know that *Jesus* is my all in all. Praise the Lord!

Through Jesus,

Barbara

11

key to power

Hello Sister!

I have just finished reading your last couple of letters, including one to Janet and am rejoicing with you!

You have passed the real crisis times; and now as the temptations come (and they surely will continue to) more and more you will identify with Jesus whom the devil tempted with his whole arsenal of temptations at once!

Imagine—he hit Him with the fleshly temptations, the pride temptations and the greed temptations—all at once! And each time Jesus was able to say, even in His weakened physical condition, *"It is written*—get thee behind me, Satan!"* (Matthew 4:1-11) Barbara, you're on the winning side—Jesus' side!

Please read I John 4:15-17 and especially pause on the 17th verse. Actually, I'm reading it in the *King James* and the *New American Standard*. The thought is so staggering that you would hesitate to write it conversationally: "As He is [Jesus] so also are we *in this world!*" How is Jesus anyway? Read Hebrews 13:8: "Jesus Christ the same yesterday, *today* and forever." And John says that God has given to each of us who are born into His family the same privileges and authority that He gave Jesus! Can you take it in?

I'm sure that means that we must study and learn God's will and His Word, as Jesus did; I'm sure it means that we will be tempted and in many ways suffer as Jesus did; I'm sure it means that we must come by experience to recognize the working of Satan and the beautiful overruling power of God in all things, as Jesus did; but it also means that *He has given us His name to use and His authority and unlimited working of the Holy Spirit as we yield more perfectly to our loving Father.*

Is that simply incredible?

Wow!

Double wow!

Dear sister, as you are growing (and the change in your letters and the episodes that you tell us are so very noticeable in their accelerating maturity) the Lord is going to use you in ways that would stagger you if you knew them now. Just rejoice and trust Him; He knows Barbara Evans—and your name is written in the Book of Life.

God bless you, sister, and we'll especially pray for you.

I love you,

Pat Boone

PB:jef

Dear Pat & Shirley,

I will make this letter brief. The Lord continues to deal with me, for which I am most thankful.

After my joyous weekend with you and sharing the experience with a few people, I became somewhat depressed (the devil, again). I knew I couldn't stay that way. Jenny Mortensen had loaned me the book *Prison to Praise*, so I started reading it. I became so involved, I couldn't even put it away for my classes at school. I read while the prof lectured.

Wow! *I had been stumbling over the key*—picked it up—dropped it and had to find it again. The last two weeks have been glorious. The devil still tries to depress me. I just start singing "Praise the Lord" or "Thank you, Lord." I pray and what a difference! One of my friends got so tickled at me because I praised the Lord for a train which was keeping us from a rehearsal. Only God knows what we were being kept from.

This key has been the source of many happy laughs and fellowship with other Christians, but I'm serious and my life has become so joyful. How many other hidden keys will I discover?

Among other things this last weekend, I was at an evangelistic meeting in a congregation where a miracle healing has taken place. Some of the people have read your book and want to discuss speaking in other tongues. I would like to meet with them, but I'm not sure how to handle it. Do you have any suggestions? I told them to read *Face Up With A Miracle* by Don Basham thinking it might help them as it did me.

Now, I must go. I have choir practice tonight. I'm so happy—I love you all so much and I thank the Lord for your friendships. I continue to pray for you and those who need your help.

Affectionately in Christ,

Barbara

12

a beginning, an end

Dear Pat,

Joyeaux Noel!

There aren't any words that I can write which truly express my love for the Boone family. Your prayers and concern for me have been a positive force in the change which God is creating. Each day I'm more thankful for His great mercy and the friends He has given me.

I am beginning to go through a process of analysis of my past. At first, it has seemed too difficult, but I know the Lord will be with me in this time of searching. I have shown my rough copy of my autobiography to my minister, and with his guidance, I have seen the necessity of trying to understand my past in order to find out who I am now.

The wonderful thing about this is that I can say, "My life is yours, Lord; and even though this may be painful, lead me through whatever may come so that in all ways I may be filled with your will and emptied of self. Nothing do I want but to live my life in complete surrender to you, my Lord and my God!"

These aren't just words, Pat. I have never meant anything so much in all my life. And even in this, I can thank the Lord, for by His grace and with the power of His Spirit, my faith continues to increase.

When I think of where I was last Christmas and what was important to me then, I rejoice that the Lord has touched my life! This Christmas, my life belongs to Jesus and I can truly be joyful in His birth.

Thank you, Pat, Shirley and girls for being a part of God's wonderful plan in my life. May He pour out His abundant love upon you and give you peace and joy this beautiful Christmas season. Amen!

Most Affectionately in Jesus,

Barbara

January 3

Dear Sister:

Happy, happy new year—in the Lord who has made them all.

I loved your letter and your card, and except for the usual hustle and bustle of the holiday, would have answered before now. As a little Christmas gift from "you-know-who," we've all been battling the bug, and finally had to take some antibiotics even though we were really praying. However, I think that we were allowed this test, because we've been praying every day with a young boy who has cancer, and has been given up by his doctors. I guess it figures that our enemy would do his best to demoralize us with a flu, while we're believing God to heal *cancer*! However, we're sticking through it, and believe that victory is in sight!

Barbara, I do encourage you to just stay close to the Lord, and in His Word, especially as you go back through the past and as we prepare the book. Continue to rejoice in what He has worked and continues to work in your life. You're very precious to us—I think you know that—and I hope that the coming year will bring opportunities for us to see you again. We'll stay in touch.

God richly bless you, sister.

Your brother in Jesus,

Pat Boone

PB:jef

January 3

Dear Brother Pat,

Tomorrow will mark *the beginning of the sixth month* since I read your beautiful story glorifying the power of God to change lives. How grateful I am to Him!

At this point, I need to tell you the latest developments so that maybe you can understand where I am now.

Before Christmas vacation, I had received an invitation from my former roommate to attend her Christmas program. Since I knew some of her choir students, it was logical that I would go. However, I felt something checking my decision to go.

To make a long story short, my friend called me from her school and almost begged me to come to the program; and then I really was convinced that I should not go. But, for some reason, I couldn't come right out and say no.

95

Well, when I started my car to leave for the afternoon party at the nursing home, my car kept dying. It died at almost every stop light and corner on the way.

So I left the party earlier than I had intended and took my car to the garage. But they couldn't work on it. I had enough time to get to my friend's house before she had to leave—*but I just couldn't go!*

Several nights later I went to bed early, thinking I would get a good night's sleep. The week had been rather difficult for me. Although it was like having Christmas for the first time, it was somewhat painful at times. The Wednesday night of that week in our prayer and Bible study, the minister asked us to express what Christmas had meant to us in the past. Most of mine had been lonely until the years with my friend, and then it seemed we almost always managed to have Christmas together. Of course, I couldn't tell all that, but I felt the memories and when we began to pray, I could not do much more than cry.

Thursday was my counseling appointment, and we got into some delicate areas to help assess my problems of the past. The counselor said my change had come *backwards to most.* Usually it's a rethinking process followed by action; *but in my case, it has been action, followed by rethinking* (or just plain "thinking").

Friday and Saturday I was busy with Christmas wrapping for friends and family. Sunday was a beautiful church experience as it always seems to be.

Sunday night I went to bed early, and the phone woke me up. It was my male gay friend with whom I had been close friends for many years. We talked in general, but he did not indicate any desire or intention to visit me, although I had invited him several times. It was a nice conversation but there was something missing. We had had a very close friendship from college days on—until I tried to explain my new way of life.

After we hung up I went back to sleep, praying that

God would take care and convince my friend of his need

I had not been asleep long when the phone rang again. It was my former roommate. She talked very coolly, and said that since I wasn't Christian enough to remember old friends and call or see them at Christmas time, she would put into words what I had been acting—that we should not call or see each other.

I was so sleepy, I couldn't think of what to say; but I think I told her that I had not thought it wise to contact her during this time that had meant so much to us, and that she was probably right—we should not see or talk to each other.

Well, when we said good-bye, it hit me like a ton of bricks—*that's the end! Wow!*

Monday I was kind of stunned, but I was all right and knew Jesus was with me. Tuesday I received a package in the mail with a note:

> Please accept this as it was purchased for you a long time ago. I would have given it to you if I had seen you, but I guess that wasn't to be. I wanted to talk to you several times but you always had to get going to some place. I hope you were awake enough last night to remember our conversation. And I might as well add that I don't think (our male friend) is being treated in a very Christian-like way either. Not if he was really the very dear friend I thought he was all these years. I guess our ideas of love of fellow man have changed considerably.... I'm not saying this to hurt you, it's only what I believe to be true. The song goes, "Make new friends but keep the old...." But I'm truly sorry you want it changed to "Make new friends, forget the old...."

I felt right away that I should answer this, but I consulted with my minister and we prayed about it first. I did write an answer:

> Thank you for the present. It was very thoughtful of you to send it.

You mentioned that you had wanted to talk to me several times. I thought I gave you the opportunity, but you didn't seem to know what to say. I can't answer questions that aren't asked, and I would never presume to force my convictions on those who do not desire them.

If it seems to you that I am not treating you in a Christian-like way, I am sorry. Yes, human kindness and concern are part of God's plan, but it doesn't always have to come with human contact. I have been and am praying for you and (our friend) in love, believing in God's promises. However, because of the nature of our past relationship, it has not been wise to have further contact. It is not because I do not care, no matter what you may be convinced to believe. *I care very deeply.* But until such time as our relationship can be of a completely different nature from that of the past, I must agree with you that it is best that we not see or talk to each other.

My deepest desire is to do God's will. My song is not "Make new friends and forget the old." It is rather, "Walk in the newness of life," and,

My friend, my friend
You're so close to my heart,
No matter what happens,
From there you'll never part.
I long so to tell you
Of all God's great love,
And how He helps each one
With His power from above.
Oh listen, my friend.
Don't turn away.
Let now be the time
To live God's way.
My friend, my friend,
You're so close to my heart,
No matter what happens,
From there you'll never part.

Good-bye, and may God, in His infinite wisdom, bless your life with His loving presence and give you His peace."

In Christ,

Barbara

98

I sent this last Thursday and I have felt such a release since then, and it seems to me that I am closer to my precious Jesus.

Of course Friday night was New Year's Eve, and I can honestly say I didn't miss the New Year's Eves of my past.

This New Year's Eve was the most beautiful and meaningful of my life. We closed the old year out with prayer and brought the New Year in with prayer.

As I drove home on New Year's Day, I sang and prayed in the Spirit as never before. And even as I felt that God was going to do something with me, this prophecy came to me:

O my child, I love thee and I will use thee in the coming year.

Fear not my power, for it will be unto thee as a light in the darkness.

This world is not your home; you're just a passing through.

I will go before thee and prepare the way that where'er ye walk, ye will know that I have been there.

I don't know the full significance of this, but it surely has strengthened me. I have felt protected and guided and loved to a certain extent in the past few months, but now I feel surrounded by the most wonderful love I have ever felt or known. I am so happy, Pat. I never want to lose this joy I have been given in the Lord.

Pat, I really don't care what the Lord wants to do with me. If I still have some things to go through in order to prepare me for the service He wants me to do, then I know He'll give me the strength to withstand the trials and temptations. I just love Him so and praise Him for His grace, mercy and unfathomable love for me. He is my all in all.

Please know that my prayers and those of others are with you and your family as you continue to serve the Lord. The Boone family and Janet are so very dear to me. I look forward to the time when we can be together, again.

Oh, how marvelous are the ways of God and how precious His binding love.

May God continue to bless you all.

With affection in Christ,

Barbara

13

"freely you've received, freely give"

Hi Barbara!

I just finished reading your letter of two days after Christmas. My heart strings were really tugging for you, but I was rejoicing by the end of the letter. You know what it reminded me of, sister? When the Holy Spirit manifested Himself to Jesus there in the Jordan River with John the Baptist and God expressed His pleasure in Christ His Son, He went out into the wilderness and was immediately tempted by the devil with the strongest possible temptation.

Here you had just been ministering the Holy Spirit and the Holy Spirit was witnessing in you and through your efforts that He was pleased with your service. *Almost*

101

immediately the strongest temptation that the devil could think of was thrown at you. He thought, as he did with Jesus, that you might be at a weak point, but having just been bolstered by the Spirit as Jesus had been, you were strong enough to withstand the temptation. And then as the angels ministered to Jesus after He resisted the temptation, so did your friends, the preacher and his family, minister to you.

Take heart, sister: God is the same and He loves you the same. Remember He said, "He who loves [even] father or mother more than me is not worthy of me." (Matthew 10:37) But those who put Him first will find that "all things" are added to them.[2]

I hope that you made contact with the Creation House people, and I feel more and more that as we get "our story" into printed form that you will experience a great spiritual harvest and your life will take on the same kind of adventure that ours has. It's almost indescribable! Happy new year, sister, and rejoice in the Lord!

Your brother,

Pat Boone

PB:jef

P.S. I wish I could travel with you a few months into the future and let you read some of the letters that will be coming to you (through the publisher) of the miraculous changes in lives brought about by the book you're working on now. You'll know then that it was worth every heartache and every anxious hour.

January 9

Dear Pat,

Thank you for sending the lovely Christmas card with the picture. I have been wishing I had a picture of the Boone family. It means a great deal to me to have it.

Last Wednesday, a week ago, I was asked to speak to a group of people concerning the gifts of the Holy Spirit, especially about a prayer language. Of course, I'm such a novice at this, I really wasn't sure of what I was doing. But, I prayed fervently about it, and prepared as well as I knew how.

After going through the Scripture references I had chosen and giving some specific examples of things that had happened to me or others I knew about, they asked me if I would be willing to pray with them. One couple left before we got down to having prayer. I feel that all of the people there were, and are, sincere about knowing more of God's will and power for their lives.

After some discussion, I told them I would be willing to pray with them. I also told them that I had prayed for God to use me in this situation according to His will and to His glorification.

When our prayer session first began, I felt prohibited from praying in my prayer language. I'm sure it was because people were listening and not praying. But as different ones began to yield themselves in prayer and pray for the concerns of their hearts, I was allowed to use my prayer language. It seemed to be directed at times to those who had just said a prayer or were in prayer. I also spoke in English some impressions that came as we were in prayer.

This was the first time I had ever spoken in English as if God were directing me. It reminded me of how Shirley spoke when we prayed together. It was a beautiful spiritual time and everyone felt a strong presence of overwhelming love.

Pat, I know that God has a plan for my life. I don't know what it is, but each day I can say more and more certainly—no matter what, my life is His. I'm much comforted tonight because of His great love, and I know

103

that I'm on my way out of this valley back to the mountain.

Please give my love to all the Boone family and Janet. I love you all so very much. May God continue to guide your steps and give you His blessed peace. I thank you that because you were willing for God to use you in an apparently "hopeless" situation, I can truly look forward to the new year with hope and an ever-deepening faith in Jesus, my Savior. God bless you all!

Your Sister in Christ,

Barbara

14

can a normal marriage be possible for me after all?

January 23

Dear Barbara:

I'm in the car on the way to the airport for another of my out-of-town trips. Shirley and Janet are sitting beside me and it's really a ludicrous scene. Here we're racing through the late afternoon traffic, hoping desperately to catch the plane, and in the eye of the hurricane I'm talking to *you!*

I did want to say an encouraging word to you though. I see so clearly—and I bet you do too—that all of the coercion and the "friendly persuasion" and pressure brought to bear on you by your former friend was all part of a spiritual battle that the devil had planned. One of the hardest things for us to realize is that *our best friends and family, if they are not discerning in*

105

the Spirit, can ask us to do the very things that would do us the most harm.

The motives aren't bad; and in fact, consciously they mean very well; but since they are not prompted by the Holy Spirit, their advice can often work to our mutual harm.

To me the best example of it all is when Jesus turned to Peter and said, "Get behind me, Satan!" (Matthew 16:23) If you'll read it, you'll see that Peter *had expressed his concern for Jesus and for His physical safety*! Jesus had said He was going into Jerusalem to be offered up, and Peter, out of human love, tried to forbid Him to go. Certainly his motives from a human standpoint were excellent and were loving. But Jesus recognized the influence of Satan in that human maneuver.

If you continue to pray for all of your friends from your past life, and occasionally send a book or some helpful spiritual food, the best thing you can possibly do in the meantime is be separate from them. If you were recovering from leprosy, you would know that the best chance for yourself and (probably your leprous friends) would be to stay a sanitary and antiseptic distance from them.

Dear sister, *Jesus has touched you and healed you of a kind of spiritual leprosy;* He longs to do the same for your friends. But the best thing you can possibly do for them is to show them that Jesus means more to you than anyone else in the world or any other association. This lesson will not be lost on them, and when *their* moments of desperation come, I firmly believe that they will follow your example and reach out to the Healer of our souls.

God bless and fill and shield you by His Spirit and in His love.

Your brother (and two sisters),

Pat Boone

PB:jef

February 11

Dear Pat,

I hope you will be as joyful over the events which I am about to relate as I am. I know that I still have much growing to do, but when I look back over the past seven months it is almost unbelievable what the Lord has done.

Thursday evening I received a call from a teacher who works with a Christian teacher friend at his school. He asked for a date for Saturday night. I said yes.

I was not apprehensive about this date. In fact, I felt very much at ease about it. Of course, I prayed concerning it—that things would go well and that the opportunity might present itself for me to be a good witness.

Well, I cannot describe to you the calm that I felt all the way through.

We went to see the movie "Fiddler on the Roof" after a nice dinner at a nearby restaurant.

When he had called, we talked for approximately two hours on the phone. One thing he asked me was who my favorite singer was, and, of course, I had to say Pat Boone. Well, I had to tell him a little, and so I took the pictures with me Saturday night and we discussed them over dinner.

After the show he brought me home, and I asked him in for a cup of tea. We talked and there was no way I could keep from talking about the Lord. He seemed extremely interested and wanted to read your book. We had gotten back to the apartment at 12:30 and he left at 2:30.

I didn't have any problems over feelings or thoughts Saturday night. Other things have come to me also.

In Sunday School I watch our minister's wife with their new baby. Just recently I have begun to think I would like to have a child of my own. *I never felt that way before.* And now, I think, for the first time in my

107

life, that I could handle a normal relationship.

Maybe it's still too soon, and I'm quite sure the Lord will take care of the situation in His own time. But for me to even *feel* like I'm ready is a miracle! *Praise the Lord!*

I don't know exactly what you think about my latest "progress report," but I do know that by the grace of God, you have introduced me to the most beautiful and precious relationship that I could ever hope to have—and that's the sweet communion with my Lord, not only in my prayer language, but also in Spirit-filled communication through the Word and in prayer.

Jesus is not just a word from the Bible. Jesus is real to me—a person present with me. Sometimes I feel so close that I think I could almost reach out with my hand and touch Him.

Oh, Pat, how I pray that I will not falter from His way. I love Him so. I want nothing more than to always be in His will.

Affectionately in Jesus,

Barbara

15

in the Spirit-filled body I find strength

Dear Pat,

For the first time since July, I have not wanted to write to you or anyone. I can't really explain why, except that maybe I have been ashamed or felt guilty about some of the things that have happened in the last couple of weeks.

I have been so exhausted and have had a temperature for several days. I've had pain like that which I had when I had a kidney and gall bladder infection. I kept believing the Lord would take care of me; now He has.

But during this time I had the strongest desires for self-satisfaction that I've ever known. I prayed and literally cried out to the Lord. He sustained me, and I thank Him for whatever reason I was being allowed these trials and for the strength He gave me to bear them.

I can't quite explain my feelings now. I continue to pray that the Lord will cleanse me, heal me and rebuke Satan from entering my thoughts and feelings. I only want to live in God's will and serve Him. This week the song, "Oh, How I Love Jesus," has continually come to me and *it is true.*

I had dinner with my parents Sunday. In the course of the conversation, I told my father that I felt I could forgive him for all that had happened when I was a teenager. Of course he didn't understand completely. Although I feel more love for my parents than in the past, I'm still not as free as I desire to be. It seems especially hard to love my father when I still feel some of the old hurts. I don't really hold them against him, but it's hard to love him.

Pat, would you especially pray that God would lead me to a Spirit-filled prayer partner. My fellowship at church is beautiful, but I feel limited by not being able to use my prayer language or share the things I feel in the Spirit.

I've really been down lately. I even thought how much better it would have been to have continued as I was than to come to this point—but I'm sure this is a lie from Satan on top of the evil thoughts which he planted.

If Satan is working so hard against me, then I have to believe that God wants to use me for something. By His Spirit, I am ready; by His love, I am willing; by His strength, I am able to do His will.

Dear brother, although this letter is full of ups and downs, I promise to write a completely joyful letter soon. I continue to rejoice in the love of my precious Jesus. He has given so much for me. I just can't tell you how much I love my Jesus tonight.

May His guiding hand be upon you and your precious family. Please know that you and all are in my prayers.

In Love through Him,

Barbara

March 5

Dear Family!

Hallelujah! Prayer has been answered. We were asking God for *a prayer partner*, and He sent me a whole church!

I was led to contact a local businessman and Christian leader. He invited me to dinner with his family. I went last Wednesday night.

I think we were all kind of stiff for a while. But I was very open and honest with them. They also had the minister of their church and his wife and daughter there for dinner.

After dinner we joined in praising the Lord and prayer. Even though I felt the presence of the Lord, I didn't feel free. I wanted to cry, but I couldn't.

When the minister and his family got ready to leave, he said something about feeling a thaw. I said yes that I had felt it, too, and still felt a brick. I had no sooner gotten the words out of my mouth than they all agreed to pray for full release for me. As I began to pray my hands reached up to heaven. It was glorious!

Well, of course, Satan moved right in and started challenging my experience. I felt very depressed Thursday afternoon. Then I remembered what my new friends of the other evening had said. It fitted so perfectly.

They had said Satan didn't want me to be strengthened by having contact with Spirit-filled Christians. They followed this up by inviting me to a Spirit-filled Catholic

111

retreat meeting that night and church services the next day.

What an experience! We were a little late for the beginning of the lesson, but we stayed for prayer and praise of the Lord. It was absolutely beautiful. I also heard the most beautiful song in the Spirit with harmony. Jesus' love was around us and in us.

Sunday morning we went to a Methodist Church before we went to the church where the pastor I had met ministers to Spirit-filled people.

I can yet hardly believe what happened to me Sunday. At this Methodist Church, the service was rather quiet. During the course of the service, the minister asked if there were any who would like to testify about what the Lord had done for their lives. I responded by singing, "He Touched Me." At the next church where we went for fellowship with Spirit-filled Christians we arrived a bit late. There is no formal service. Although the teaching comes first, they are open to let the Spirit move. I have never felt so free in my life. They had a time of sharing, witnessing, praise and prayer. During this time there was a message from God in another language which was interpreted by the minister.

Since I had met the minister, he called on me and asked if I would testify and sing "He Touched Me." I have never experienced anything like it! My voice was not my own, and I just hugged the people sitting nearest me on the way back to my seat. There were other testimonies which made the presence of the Lord so very real.

I told you about two letters ago, that one of these times I would be able to write a completely joyful letter. *Well, this is it.* Joyful!

Now, my dear, dear family in L.A., I just want you to know how very thankful I am for you all. I continue to pray that God will be with you, strengthen you and guide you.

I remember how Shirley said she felt that the Lord

would work with me very quickly. As I look back and see that *it has been only eight months*, I can't help but rejoice in the Lord's goodness. It is sometimes difficult to even remember what my life was like before and impossible to imagine it without the Lord as my Savior and Guide.

I love you all—may God bless you in a special way!

In Him,

Barbara

16

battle of giants

Dear Pat,

Things are happening so fast that I can hardly keep up with them. I know it's been awhile since I have written, so this will probably be a book.

Since I have been in the fellowship of Spirit-filled Christians, I have felt the need to read the Word and pray more. However, I haven't been able to comprehend what I read.

Recently, I went to a Christian fellowship dinner and meeting. I asked for special prayer. I really didn't feel anything, *but I know something happened.* My mind has been more clear, and I even had a private teaching session with our pastor after church Sunday. Previously

115

what he said was too deep for me, but I was able to comprehend most of it this time. I really want to be able to understand the Word of God.

I've left the other church now, and I'm attending the meetings and church services of this Spirit-filled fellowship. I've met so many terrific people.

The pastor is often commenting on new books about the move of the Holy Spirit. I've just finished *Like A Mighty Wind* by Mel Tari. It's terrific! I shared part of it with a young Bible college girl who has been seeking for a deeper relationship with God and has questioned the idea of prayer language. We had a wonderful time sharing together. I'm sure she will go back to Bible college with some new ideas.

Sunday night my younger brother and a friend of his were at church. My brother has been attending services with me occasionally since last October, but he really hasn't made a commitment to the Lord.

But the Lord really moved in this service. There was a young couple there who had visited with the pastor and his family during the day. This young man, Jim, had been delivered from a life of crime and has been having difficulty finding and keeping a job. He and his wife have both accepted the Lord, but aren't sure what road they're on.

I feel that the Lord has His hands on their lives. My brother was impressed by Jim's story, because he himself has gotten into some pretty tight corners! So he could really appreciate what Jim said. That was a beautiful meeting!

You know, Pat, it's so hard for me to imagine where I was almost nine months ago. "Old things are passed away, all things are become new!" (2 Corinthians 5:17)

Your letters mean a great deal more to me than words can express. However, I do know from several sources that your work load is almost unbelievable, so I do not expect you to write to me as you did in the beginning. You know how very much I *needed* it then. I still need all the spiritual food I can get from all my Spirit-filled brothers and sisters, but the Lord has provided a group of His family members to help me. Now, you must have others who need your attention as I did in the beginning.

I know I have not yet attained, and that I am only striving toward that final goal. But Jesus has shown me the Way through your first efforts. You'll never know how many people I have met in my singing who have read *A New Song* and have had a life-changing experience with Jesus. Praise God!

The Lord has given me such peace and calm tonight. I feel His Presence and His Love around me in an indescribably beautiful way. "His banner over us is Love!" (Song of Solomon 2:4)

Your Sister in Christ,

Barbara

April 1

Wow! I just got home from a prayer meeting where I found out *my brother asked Jesus to come into his heart*. Tears of joy come to me even as I just praise the Lord for this. You should have seen me when he gave his testimony of how Jesus came into his heart and how he loves Jesus. Hallelujah!

My brother has already been used in an unusual way to help a friend of his, Larry. Larry is about twenty-one years old, but seemingly has the mentality of a ten-year old. He came with my brother to one of the first prayer meetings I attended of this Spirit-filled fellowship.

My brother has been praying and reading the Bible with Larry. Larry's parents and mine got tired of the boys running around together constantly. I think my parents thought Larry was a bad influence on my brother, and didn't realize that my brother might be a good influence on Larry.

The boys came to the prayer meeting, and Larry looked wild. Jim, the young man I mentioned earlier, spotted Larry's reactions as being typical of a person on drugs. *He was right; Larry was high on L.S.D.* I don't mind telling you, I was shocked. I've never seen anything like this. We really got busy praying and rebuking Satan and his demon powers.

Jim had been through withdrawal before and had seen others on L.S.D. He recommended that Larry be taken to the hospital. The Lord worked through Jim in a beautiful way to keep Larry from tripping out.

I have to say that the Lord has surely been protecting Larry. If he hadn't come to this meeting, I shudder to think what would have happened to him. Praise God for His marvelous love and tender mercies!

When the men got back from taking Larry to the hospital, I felt led to share my story, especially with Jim. My brother had gone home so he could tell Larry's parents that he was staying over and would be home some time the next day.

As Jim and I talked we realized that our deliverances are both no less miraculous. His story is much the same as that of another man which you related to me. Only through God could *any* of us have been delivered. Praise Him!

The next day, I met Jim and we went out to talk with Larry's parents. Jim had already taken Larry home, but no one was there at the time. When we got there, Larry's parents still were not home, so we waited for them outside and prayed while we waited.

I have never experienced anything such as I am about to relate. When his parents got out of the car, they did not stop, speak, or even acknowledge our presence. I've never felt such an "icy wind." We asked Larry to introduce us, but he was reluctant. We told him that we wanted to give them the name of a doctor and a free clinic where people who were concerned could help him.

Jim and I finally went up to the house and started

to tell Larry's mother who we were and what we wanted. She told us she didn't have time for us. We told her we were there to help Larry and she started a tirade of foul language, cursing us—telling us that Larry just made these suicide threats to get attention.

She even said Larry had threatened suicide so many times that she gave him a gun or some other tool to see if he would do it. Larry has cut his wrists several times and has horrible scars to show for it.

Finally she said she was going to send Larry to an asylum because she couldn't put up with him any longer.

"Can we take him with us?" Jim asked.

"No," she said. "I have *always* taken care of him, and I'll *continue* to take care of him."

All the time we were talking, Larry's father sat at the table, not saying a word.

Jim and I finally asked if we could pray for them, and Larry's mother and she didn't care *what* we did. So Jim and I clasped hands and he prayed silently while I prayed aloud. I surely felt the Spirit move as we prayed.

When we finished praying, Larry's mother seemed more willing to listen to us about the clinic. Only the Lord could have calmed her down because she had been so hostile.

We visited Larry several times more during the following week. Finally his parents reluctantly allowed him to go to church with us.

During the service we had special prayer for Larry and felt strongly that the Lord had really touched him and delivered him from some of Satan's demonic powers. Larry's story reminds me of the man in the tombs who cut himself with stones in Mark 5.

The next few nights we went to Larry's to pray with him. Larry said he had actually seen demons in his room. His mother even told us that they had heard strange sounds in the house at different times.

Now, *what I am about to tell you seems so unreal that*

119

it could have come straight out of a science fiction story.

One night Jim and I went over to visit Larry. When we rang the doorbell his mother came to answer. She gave us a rough time about interfering. We told her we only came because Larry called us to come and pray with him. She finally agreed that he could come out to the car so that we could pray together.

Larry told us that the devil had appeared in his room the night before. We prayed and believed God for further deliverance and healing for Larry. At one point Jim said he heard something outside the car and we both felt an evil presence. Later, as we were talking about this, I said I had had the feeling that the car was going to start rocking. Jim said he had had the same conviction. We rebuked Satan in the Name of Jesus; and the Lord touched Larry again while we were praying for him.

When we got out of the car to walk Larry back to the house, we prayed all the way. I seemed as though during the whole approach back to the house we were wading through evil spirits. Do you know how walking through a field of tall weeds feels? Well, our experience was like that, but we couldn't actually see or feel anything.

When we related these happenings to our pastor and some of the other Spirit-filled members of our fellowship, they had no trouble believing the incident was true, because they have been in this walk longer than Jim, Karen and I. Praise God, He is the victor!

Although we have continued to pray for Larry, his mother has now forbidden him to see any of us. I feel so sorry for him. I'm sure he doesn't really understand all that has happened or is happening to him. We realize it's best just to leave him in the Lord's hands.

I've tried to be as honest as I can in writing all of this. I hope it will make some kind of sense to you.

May God continue to bless you all and keep you safe in His care.

Love in Jesus,

Barbara

Hello dear sister!

This last "book" of yours is really spine-tingling and it makes me praise God for your growth and beseech Him for your protection. I know that you are under severe attack, but doesn't it thrill you to realize that you have become somebody very special *both to God and to the devil*! You know who's going to win, don't you? Hallelujah!

The resistance of Larry's mother is a perfect parallel to the apostle Peter's attempted roadblock of Jesus in Matthew 16. She thinks she's helping her son, but is being used by Satan to block God's will. *Like Jesus, let's rebuke the devil in His name!*

I've taken the liberty of sending that last communication of yours to a friend who is a real prayer warrior and whose hackles rise, just like mine, when the devil manifests himself so obviously and so recklessly. He may want to call you and pray with you—to encourage you in the kind of warfare we get into when we really step out for the Lord.

We love you, gal—keep on singing, praying and just *being* the daughter of the Living God!

Your brother,

Pat Boone

PB:jef

17

"and the truth shall make you free"

Dear Pat,

Praise the Lord in the beauty of His Holiness!

Some of my friends and I have been working with young people who have been on dope or involved in witch-craft or have sex hangups. The pastor of our fellowship, my brother Jim and his wife and I have been meeting with some of these young people in a nearby town lately.

One afternoon I didn't go to the meeting, and Jim called me to say he was with a 16-year-old boy by the name of Allan who was a homosexual, and would I come over and meet him. I went to Jim and Karen's house and we talked. After he realized that the power of God working in a life *can* change a person even from a condition as hopeless as homosexuality, he really wanted to know Jesus.

We prayed with Allan and immediately a noticeable change came over him even in the way he talked. We went from Jim's to a meeting of other young people, acquaintances Allan had made earlier that day. They could *see* that Jesus had touched his life and that he was changed. All of this was emphasized several weeks later when Allan was baptized in the Holy Spirit. Now his life also radiates the love of Christ.

We have also been working with a young man who has been deeply involved in witchcraft. The Lord has delivered him, but he can't seem to stay free. We are still praying for him and believing God for the answer.

Praise God for the way He is working. One of the teachers asked me to talk to him and his wife. They have been considering "joining a church." When I shared with them, they said we had talked more about Jesus in that one evening than all the times put together when they attended church membership classes. We had a beautiful time together. But I know the Lord still has to deal with their hearts. Pray for us, please.

More love in Jesus,

Barbara

May 27

Dear Pat,

You know, Pat, I have had a wonderful feeling that things were going to happen in my life, soon. The Lord has assured me that I will have a Spirit-filled husband, for *I really desire to have a home and family* and live in the unity of God's Spirit and love.

Recently, I have spent a great deal of the time with

our pastor's daughter, Gina. We shared our needs and desires as well as some of our past heartaches and how the Lord was working with us.

One message which has really gotten through to me is how God wants us to love Him. We are all the time expecting Him to love us and forget that He made us for Himself. Gina and I have talked about this several times. Then one night God gave Gina a message for me.

"My child, do not be afraid to let me love you. I want to bathe you in my love; I want to swathe you in my love; I want my love to flow through you to reach a lost and dying world."

Afterward, the room seemed filled with the presence of God. What I received was like a baptism in love. We discussed the real need for people to just love God—to worship Him and praise Him.

The following Sunday was one of the most beautiful experiences of my life. It seemed like the whole service was directed toward how much God loves us and wants us to love Him.

There were several testimonies, and the Lord used different members of the body to minister to the needs of others. It seemed like the only song we could sing was "Jesus Loves Me, This I Know." The Lord impressed upon me that we must come to Him as little children.

Monday I went to school rejoicing and still feeling "mentholated," although I was physically tired. The children even seemed different to me. I could almost see into or through them to the divine spark which God has planted in each one.

In the afternoon, I received a phone call from Gina. She said my brother had become ill and was taken to the hospital. She said he could go home and asked if I wanted to pick him up after school.

After school I went to get my brother to take him home, and Gina went with us. When we got home, my parents were really upset. My dad started talking to my brother and gave him a rough time about all this "religious stuff." They blamed his friends for his getting sick. Then my father started in on me about this "crazy religion" I'd gotten into—how I wasn't the same.

I had been praying silently in the Spirit, but then I realized I was beginning to react. I excused myself and went to another room. There I prayed for the Lord to take full command of this situation, and I thanked Him for doing so and for the lessons we would learn from it.

Back with the others again, I heard Gina ask if she could pray before we left. At this *I began to feel such a tremendous love for my father.* It was almost as if someone had lit a fire inside of me. Yet, I felt reluctant to go to him. I did go to my mother. I told her that I loved her whether she loved me or not and whether or not she understood what I was doing.

She said softly, "Keep praying."

I hugged her gently and went back to where I had been standing between Gina and my dad. My father asked my mother if she wanted Gina to pray, and she said yes.

Gina's prayer must have been by the Holy Spirit. It was beautiful! One thing really got through—she thanked God for the wonderful love He had given her for my mother and especially my father. Wow!

The fire of love inside me exploded! When she finished, *I went to my father,* put my arms around him and told him I loved him very much, just as I had told my mother.

I told him that the Lord had given me forgiveness in my heart for him earlier this year, but I still hadn't been able to love him as I should. When we finally left, I was truly rejoicing—for God has given me love in my heart for my father. The whole situation had been in the Lord's hands.

In my thinking about this situation now, I feel that one reason I had difficulty accepting the love which God has for me was because I did not have a good father image.

126

It was a fear image rather than love image.

Isn't it beautiful that when I accepted God's love and verbally acknowledged it that He bathed me in a wonderful flow of love which allowed me to love my father for the first time I can remember since I was a small child? Praise our wonderful Lord and Savior!

Tuesday was another beautiful day. I felt that I wanted to call on *my former roommate.* I had some money which I still owed her, and I wanted to take it to her in person.

We talked for a while about school. Finally, the conversation got around to Jesus. Before leaving I asked if I could pray. She said I could if I wished to. So, I prayed for her and then hugged her. It was a hug in the purity of God's wonderful love! Hallelujah! *I'm really free!*

Pat, do you remember that in your first letter you said God would purify my love for my friend? Then Gina's message for me was that God wanted to purify me in His love. *For the first time in ten years I was able to hug the one whom I had loved in the flesh in the purity of God's love. Praise the Almighty and Everlasting God!*

No one can realize what a tremendous change has come about in my life. Since I was 18, I was obsessed with the desire to love and be loved by my friend. I went through years of torture—waiting, hoping, believing and even praying that someday the love I felt deep within would be returned. In all that time I never knew that the person I was really searching for was Jesus Christ, the Son of the Living God. Only when God opened my eyes which had been blinded by Satan did I discover that there was something desperately wrong in my life. When I finally admitted it and gave up my life, I found what my whole being had craved and ached for—Jesus! Praise God that "ye shall know the truth, and the truth shall make you free."

Oh, Pat, *it is so important that people who have a homosexual hang-up realize that Jesus is their only answer.* The Lord has shown me through a series of events and miracles in my life that *a deliverance from past resentments, hatreds, and unforgiving attitudes is essential.* As long as I had unconfessed sins, unforgiveness, and wrong attitudes, *I was vulnerable to the enemy because he was still holding ground within me.*"

A friend was talking to me one evening about having every area of our lives covered by the blood of Jesus. In other words, all secret sins or hidden wrong attitudes should be brought into the open and confessed. As long as they remain hidden, the enemy has ground to stand on in our lives. When they are brought out into the open and confessed, the blood of Jesus cleanses every stain. And Satan is banished!

When we were discussing this, I received an impression of a demon running away from me. Although I gave my life to the Lord, at times I suffered from attacks of the enemy which were almost more than I could bear. Through counseling and being willing to let pride go by the wayside, the Lord has revealed areas of my life that I had not even remembered. Praise His Name!

Oh Pat, I know I can't go only part of the way. Jesus said in Matthew 10:39, "He who has found his life shall lose it; and he who has lost his life for My sake *shall find it.*" I must be willing to lose my whole self in Jesus, and His life in me will become the true life.

I know that I have not yet come to the place where I can be all that God wants me to be, but now I'm free! I'm free in Jesus. He has changed my desires so completely that I look forward to the fulfillment of His promise that He will send me a Spirit-filled husband.

Jesus must come before anything and anyone in my life. But I know that in God's divine plan, woman was created for man. There is to be a unity in the Spirit between a man and a woman so that they are truly one, a complete personality.

Someday soon, I shall know that completeness.

Well, Pat, I cannot praise the Lord enough for you and your precious family. I pray that He will keep you, guide you and bless you as you continue to serve Him. I love you all!

Love in Jesus,

Barbara

P.S.

Recently, I had the joy of returning to the place where I met Jesus. It is impossible to describe in words the scene. The rock on which I sat while I was searching the Scriptures for the truth and the bank of the stream with the wild flowers and trees being reflected in the water provided an atmosphere for worship and adoration to God. As I lay on the rock, not being able to remember the feeling of hopelessness I had had a year ago, I knew that deep within my heart I had a desire that had not faded but grown more intense. My desire is to be filled with Jesus. Jesus is the One for whom I long had sought. This song tells the story of that day a year ago.

I SEARCHED FOR THEE

One stormy day I searched for Thee
O God, to find Thy will for me.
My sin was great, a heavy load
For me to carry down life's road.

I sat beside the cooling stream
And cried and prayed to be redeemed.
I felt that all in Thee was well,
But for my life, I could not tell.

And then I walked back through the field,
My burden heavy, then I kneeled
To pray and give my life to Thee,
My heart ached deep; my tears flowed free.

Your healing hand upon my brow
Raised me up and showed me how
To lose my sin and all my pain,
Eternal life that I might gain.

O thank you for your Spirit, Lord,
And Christ who came to be adored,
But left His glory all with Thee
To be hung upon the tree.

In Him is Life and Light and Peace,
And from our sin, a full release
With great assurance for the day
He'll come to take us all away.

All glory to Thy Holy Name!
All praise to Thee who art the same
Each day, each week, each year, each hour.
Oh, thank Thee for Thy cleansing power. Amen!

Agape,

Barbara

June 12

Hi Sister!

I could never hope to match that last letter of yours,
and I won't even try. Janet and I had both been wondering
why we hadn't heard from you in so long, but now we
know. Boy, do we know!

I pray for you quite often, as you can imagine, and
my prayer always is that God will strengthen you with
might and intervene by His Spirit. I hope you'll be able
to record what God has done for you, so that others
may begin to benefit by your story. Perhaps you've seen,
as I have, an avalanche of books coming out now on
homosexuality, excusing and "understanding" and almost
(and indeed actually) *encouraging* homosexuality in today's world. Your story needs to be on the newsstands

today; however, the Lord is in charge and His timing is perfect.

We all send our love and I feel reasonably sure that during the summer as we travel we'll probably see you. God love and bless you richly.

Your brother,

Pat

PB:jef

P.S. I'll bet a husband is on the way! But be cautious and commit that especially to the Lord.

postscript

by Pat Boone

It was a warm morning in July when my secretary Janet came to my home with the mail.

"You may want to shoot me for this," she said, handing me a neatly hand-written letter with a woman's signature, "but this woman phoned the office the other day and sounded so desperate that I told her if she wrote you a letter I thought you'd answer it. And here it is."

Like other entertainers who appear on TV, in motion pictures, and whose stories and pictures appear in movie magazines, I receive a good bit of fan mail. But I had never read a letter quite like this one.

The girl, Barbara Evans (alias Joy Carol), said she was 27—and a lesbian. And while she claimed to be "happily married," it was obvious also that she was disturbed.

She had read the book I had recently written, *A New Song*, in which I related my own story of entrapment by the world, self-concern and the devil—and my escape.

While she didn't say so in so many words, it was obvious that she also felt trapped in her world—and wondered if there *was* an escape for her!

"Can you help me?" she asked.

Well, you don't have to be around the entertainment profession long to discover that it is peopled by quite a few lesbians and homosexuals. So I have had my share of contacts with them, many times on a very friendly basis.

My impression had always been that they were irrevocably committed to their way of life. They might vascillate between partners, but once they have become homosexual they seldom, if ever, become totally heterosexual again.

So, like many other Americans in recent years I have really been deeply concerned by the increased pervasiveness of homosexuality in our society. The much publicized "Gay In" gathering in Manhattan's Central Park in 1971, with similar small demonstrations in other cities, seemed to me to provide fresh evidence of the decadence of the society in which we live. At the same time, I was aware that Kinsey's famous study, *Sexual Behavior in the Human Male* of twenty-four years ago, claimed that even then *37 percent of U.S. men were inclined toward homosexuality!* [1] What was happening to our society? We seemed to be rushing openly toward a Sodom-like culture that encouraged three or four "sexes" —with the resulting chaos and eventual disease, disaster and ruin.

Now I was being asked by a lesbian for help. What could I do?

Well, I knew that a number of books had been published on the subject. In the well-known book *Strange Loves*, an English physician Dr. Ustace Chesser attempts to humanize the homosexual for the general public. Other books by Dr. Paul Rosenfels and Dr. Judd Marmor call for a more sympathetic understanding of the subject.

Stage plays and movies in recent months have bombarded us with homosexual themes and actions—from *Zachariah*, the homosexual western, to *Loot* where a homosexual pass was made and accepted, to *Midnight Cowboy, Women in Love, The Fox, The Damned*, and countless others. Television too has taken its turn at presenting both the homosexual and the lesbian as increasingly accepted members of today's society. Now they're starting to show the films too—some that were rated "X"!

Most comedians today have a "fag bit" as a standard part of their acts. But communications techniques—the press, TV, movies—only reflect public opinion and mores. They don't make recommendations.

What do medical authorities have to say?

"Whether it is considered congenital or acquired, homosexuality is an activity that does nobody any harm. It is not a social crime," [2] Dr. Wilhelm Reich, the psychologist says.

Dr. Marcel Saghir of the Washington University School of Medicine in St. Louis asserts, "Neurotic illness is not significantly different between homosexual and heterosexual men, provided they are of similar age and socio-economic status." [3]

The only trouble with these assertions is that in our attempt to understand the homosexual or lesbian—we often look only at the externals—the natural man. And man cannot be considered as two dimensional. He is body and mind—*but he is also spirit*. And it is only when man's *spirit* is in the proper relationship with God that he becomes a completely happy, well-adjusted person.

There's one great source of information on things of the Spirit; does the Bible have anything to say about the lesbian and the homosexual?

In the New Testament Paul wrote by divine inspiration to a group of Christians in the church at Rome describing those who had turned away from God.

Therefore God gave them over in the lusts of their hearts to impurity, that their bodies might be dishonored among them . . . they exchanged the truth of God for a lie, and worshiped and served the creature rather than the Creator . . . For this reason God gave them over to degrading passions; for their women exchanged the natural function for that which was unnatural, and in the same way also the men abandoned the natural function of the woman and burned in their desire towards one another, men with men committing indecent acts and *receiving in their own persons the due penalty of their error* (Romans 1:24-27). Also read 1 Corinthians 6:9, 10.

Plainly, from the biblical point of view, the homosexual act is considered more than sin in the sight of God. It is a fatal disease!

Two burning questions therefore remain: one, what is the cause of homosexuality? Two, is there a cure?

Dr. Mary Calderone, co-founder and executive director of the Sex Information and Educational Council of the U.S., says, "While parents, of course, have a great deal to do with how a child turns out, many other factors and environmental influences, such as a child's peers and experiences and other adults, can affect her or him as well. *Homosexuals come out of as many different kinds of homes as heterosexuals do.*" [4]

In a recent issue of *Redbook* two psychologists, two psychiatrists and one sociologist were asked the question, "What are the key factors in a woman's early upbringing that may predispose her to find sex with another woman?" [5]

They were divided in their opinion into two general categories. One group took the position that homosexuality is not a pathological state but simply another way of expressing a loving relationship. Those who championed this position did not believe an effort should be made to change.

The other group held the more generally accepted view that lesbianism like male homosexuality stems from *a fear of the opposite sex*. They asserted that lesbians

136

have a "background history of a disturbed relationship with both parents, specifically in areas that affect normal sexual maturation." [6]

The mothers of these lesbians are usually described as domineering, competitive and show a contempt for their daughter's femininity. Often they have a son whom they prefer and to whom they give the majority of their attention and affection. A twist to this type of mother is the one who attempts to desexualize her daughter in order to maintain her as a lifelong companion.

Fathers too can contribute to a tendency on the part of a daughter to lesbianism. One type may object to and criticize his daughter's boyfriends, or he may play an overly attentive role, inappropriately intimate, preferring his daughter to his wife.

The other type of father is "unprotective, apparently detached, and afraid of antagonizing his wife and so abandons his daughter to his mate." [7]

So, although the contributing factors vary in each homosexual's personal story, the basic *cause* of homosexuality seems to be an imbalance at home: a lack of love and wise discipline from both parents. It invariably stems from a home situation in which God's blueprint for living has either been ignored or twisted out of shape.

Twisted lives are the result.

What hope then is there for the homosexual? Humanly speaking, not much. So little progress has been made, in fact, that the trend in medical circles today is to attempt to help the homosexual to *adjust* to his homosexuality *rather than to help him escape from it.*

Yet in Barbara's letters we have a factual account of how a commitment to God by a young woman has led directly, miraculously, to her *deliverance from the desire* to sin in this self-destroying way.

In the Bible passage referred to earlier (Romans 1), the apostle Paul is speaking to the citizens of the nation of Rome at its supremacy—but at a point in time where the cracks in its bastions are beginning to appear. While it achieved great military goals, made enormous judicial contributions to the world and perhaps had become the wealthiest nation in recorded history, internal moral corruption had begun to eat at its vitals. So Paul, the author of the book of Romans, warns a group of young Christians against the dire punishment for the sin of homosexuality.

Sodomy, as well as every other conceivable perversion, was openly accepted.

God hasn't changed His mind, or His hatred of evil.

But the wonderful feature of God's plan for man is that no matter what his sin may be—nor how far it may have separated him from God—*there is a way* this ruptured relationship may be restored. It is God's desire, His longing, that man may come to experience a vital, intimate relationship with Him.

Solomon, the wisest man who ever lived, said, "There is a way *which seems* right to a man, but its end is the way of death." (Proverbs 14:12) From Adam until now, man has followed his own instincts, his own intellect, his own desires, trying to "get the most out of life," on his own terms, and in ways that seem right to him.

Men seem willing to try almost *any* way—except God's way!

And tragically, heartbreakingly, the price for traveling these other ways is disease and death. And not just for homosexuals! This is a description of the human condition, of every individual separated from God—either by the circumstances of his early life or by his own wilful disobedience and sin.

But there is a cure!

For this raging epidemic of self-destruction, of spiritual blindness, of moral cancer, of life-wasting, personality-warping disease, there is one perfect antibody: the sinless blood of Jesus!

When He walked the earth as the humble son of a Nazarene carpenter, Jesus kept reminding all who heard

138

Him that their main responsibility in life was to *love God with all their hearts, minds and souls*—and then to love their neighbors without reserve. He showed them perfectly how it was done, and as a result His life sparked miracles everywhere He went.

Because He loved God with a total submission, Jesus could draw upon the power of the Holy Spirit to transform people physically and spiritually. And He still does it!

He *still* says, "Come to me, and I'll give you peace. Come to me, and I'll give you joy. Come to me, and let me give you life! Let me love you, with a perfect love! And then, if you love me—keep my commandments. My commandments will keep you from death. Let me teach you how to live, and to live abundantly!"

In John 15:11 He says, "These things I have spoken to you, that My joy may be in you, and that your joy may be made full."

Joy!

Do you see it? Jesus—God made flesh—became our teacher, our example, and our Way to life, love and joy! As the truly great Physician, He met spiritual disease with compassion, not condemnation. To the woman taken in the very act of adultery He said, "Neither do I condemn you; go your way; from now on, sin no more."

Neither did He condemn Zaccheus, the little Jewish tax collector who'd been swindling his own people. In Luke 19, Jesus invited Himself to Zaccheus' house; and in the intimate presence of the Son of God, the tax collector was transformed!

"For the Son of Man has come to seek and to save that which was lost." (Luke 19:10)

Read the story of Levi (or Matthew) in Luke 5: 27-32. He too was a tax collector, despised by his own people; but Jesus chose him as an apostle with two words: "Follow me." And this man wrote the first book in the New Testament!

He was transformed by his relationship with Jesus. Hear the Savior's gentle answer when He was criticized by the religious leaders of His day for eating and drinking with notorious sinners, prostitutes, lepers and scoundrels: "It is the sick who need a doctor, not those in good health. My purpose is to invite sinners to turn from their sins, not to spend my time with those who think themselves already good enough." (Luke 5:31, 32, *Living Bible*)

Yes, homosexual sister or brother—there is a cure.

Jesus.

"Look! A leper is approaching. He kneels before Him, worshiping. 'Sir,' the leper pleads, "If you want to, you can heal me."

"Jesus touches the man. 'I want to,' He says, 'be healed.' And instantly the leprosy disappears." (Matthew 8:1-3, *Living Bible*)

Jesus *wants* to heal the sick, physically and spiritually. But the one who comes to Him must know he's sick—and confess it—and like the leper, worship his Lord.

Barbara Evans came to Jesus like the leper. She was aware of her desolation; she quickly and humbly knelt before the Son of God; and she experienced His miraculous touch.

Oh, she'd been living a comfortable enough life—but it didn't satisfy her innermost needs. And she was willing to pay whatever the price to find the better way.

Some may object that Barbara's journey from practicing lesbianism is too simple. In many ways it *is* incredible. But facts are stubborn.

Remember a couple of fantastic things from her letters: something the psychological counselor told Barbara—and something she told me.

The counselor told Barbara that her change "had come *backwards* to most. Usually it's a re-thinking process followed by action; but in my case, *it has been action, followed by re-thinking!*"

Grasp it? Psychiatry tries to peel away the layers, painfully, one by one, hoping to get back to the "primal scream." But Jesus *starts on the inside*, motivating

140

action, creating a new personality from within. Only God Himself can do that.

And then, remember what Barbara told me about her father: "Isn't it beautiful that when I accepted God's love and verbally acknowledged it that He bathed me in a wonderful flow of love *which allowed me to love my father* for the first time I can remember since I was a small child?"

Again the healing touch of the Master Physician.

The lack of a loving relationship with her father contributed largely to her becoming a homosexual in the first place. God knew that. When Barbara gave her heart to Jesus, He brought her gently back to her father.

And then, immediately, He gave her an opportunity to be with her former homosexual mate again. This time, she could truly love and pray for and hug her friend "in the purity of God's wonderful love."

She was *free!* Like the leper, Jesus had healed Barbara, from the inside out.

First, give your life completely to Jesus. Claim the promises He has made to *you.*

Then determine to worship and obey Him, fully expecting your real enemy, Satan, to harass, tempt and threaten you. He *will!* But you'll soon come to know, by personal experience, that *"greater is He that is in you*—than he that is in the world."

You'll quickly discover as I have, as Barbara Evans has, and as hundreds of thousands of other men and women across the U.S. and around the world are experiencing—*Jesus is the greatest power in the universe.* He, and He alone, can bring you that precious inner peace; He *is* the fulfillment you have sought so long.

Oh yes—the promises. Dear friend, the whole Bible, from Genesis to Revelation, is one long list of promises. In Genesis 1:26-30, we see that *everything in this world* was meant for the faithful servant of God, with the precious companionship of God in the bargain! That's what He wants for us today, and our task is to get back gradually into that relationship with our Father who creates and provides all things.

Of course, the Number One promise of all is the one that restores an individual to that state God created him for: "As many as received Him, *to them gave He power to become the sons of God,* even to them that believe on His name." (John 1:12)

"For God loved the world so much that He gave His only Son so that anyone who believes in Him shall not perish but have eternal life."

"God did not send His Son into the world to condemn it—but to save it." (John 3:16 and 17, *Living Bible*)

After you are born again by His Holy Spirit into God's family—and this occurs when you kneel in His presence and give Him your heart in submission and obedience —He begins to *flood* you with promises that stagger your comprehension! Listen:

"Those who believe and are baptized will be saved. But those who refuse to believe will be condemned.

"And those who believe shall use my authority to cast out demons, and they shall speak new languages. They will be able even to handle snakes with safety, and if they drink anything poisonous, it won't hurt them; and they will be able to place their hands on the sick and heal them." (Mark 16:16-18, *Living Bible*)

"If you only have faith in God—this is the absolute truth—you can say to this Mount of Olives, 'Rise up and fall into the Mediterranean,' and your command will be obeyed. All that's required is that you really believe and have no doubt!

"Listen to me! You can pray for *anything*, and *if you believe, you have it*; it's yours! But when you are praying, first forgive anyone you are holding a grudge against, so that your Father in heaven will forgive you your sins too." (Mark 11:22-25, *Living Bible*)

"And Peter replied, 'Each one of you must turn from sin, return to God, and be baptized in the name of Jesus Christ for the forgiveness of your sins; *then you also shall receive this gift, the Holy Spirit.* For Christ promised him to each one of you who has been called by the Lord our God, and to your children and even to those in distant lands!" (Acts 2:38-39, *Living Bible*)

Do you need the overcoming, victorious power of the Holy Spirit in your life? Read Ephesians 1:13, John 7:37-39, Luke 11:10-13, Romans 8:1 and 2—in fact, just read the whole eighth chapter of Romans for most fantastic list of promises ever made!

Oh friend, read Matthew 5, 6, and 7 and hear the incredible promises from Jesus' own lips that *every material and spiritual need* will be supplied for the trusting child of God! It's true!

Read John 8:32, Galatians 5:22, 23, Hebrews 9:15 and 10:36; *read* 1 Timothy 4:8, Proverbs 3:7-10, Philippians 4:19, Mark 10:28-30; *read* Isaiah 54 through 61:3, John 14, 15 and 16, and Ephesians 3:16-20 for a mind-boggling assortment of blessings *promised* to the brother or sister of Jesus the King!

Read in 1 Corinthians 10:13 that *no temptation* will confront you without *God's personal provision* of a way of escape—and in Hebrews 1:13-14 that *angels* will be sent to minister to *you!*

Dear brother, dear sister, get your Bible and read your inheritance from your living Father! I haven't even scratched the surface here!

Do you understand now why Barbara and I call our story *JOY?*

Because that's what it *is*—a story of fulfillment, excitement, of healing and transformation, of miraculous, God-given joy!

"For you have a new life. It was not passed on to you from your parents, for the life they gave you will fade away. This new one will last forever, for it comes from Christ, God's ever-living Message to men." (1 Peter 1:23, 24, *Living Bible*)

Her letters clearly reveal both the desperate inward struggle that took place, the growing awareness of the joy of her deliverance, and the exuberance of Barbara's new relationship with God through Jesus the Christ.

I don't know how it affects you, but I weep again when I feel her enthusiasm *as she shares her new life with those around her.*

And if I were to attempt to evaluate the various factors which have been at play in this drama of a changing life, I believe I'd rate this near the top.

Of course, Barbara has suffered discouragements and faced setbacks along the way. But each time, as she turns to the Word of God, she finds the mighty promises she needs with which to meet the temptations. And as she acts upon these promises, experiences their reality and then shares the results with others, she discovers that new moral strength is flowing in her. This in turn produces an overflowing joy which engulfs her and those around her.

Beautiful!

No matter who you are—a practicing lesbian, homosexual, or one troubled with such thoughts—this is hope for you. I'm telling you that what God has done for Barbara Evans, He can also do for you. And He *wants* to!

---

[1] *Saturday Review*, Feb. 12, 1972, p. 24.

[2] *Ibid.*, p. 26.

[3] *Ibid.*, p. 26.

[4] *Redbook*, Nov. 1971, p. 84.

[5] *Ibid.*, p. 192.

[6] *Ibid.*, p. 195.

[7] *Ibid.*, p. 195.

45833

ook may be kept